AF697453

Spending Grandma's Inheritance

To Cookie,
Thank you for training
Blaire. She thinks highly
of you. Good luck,
Mark Fisher
5/25/11

J. Mark Fisher

Copyright © 2005 by J. Mark Fisher

All rights reserved. No part of this book may be reproduced
in any form without written permission from the publisher.

Published by J. Mark Fisher

ISBN: 0-9770262-0-5

Printed in Canada

Contents

Stories

Two Generations

My Story

Disclaimer

Although the facts surrounding the stories in this book are true, the names, places and sequence of events have been changed to make the stories easier to read and protect confidential information. No legal action should be taken as a result of reading one of these stories or the legal analysis that follows. You should rely solely upon a lawyer representing you from your own state who is familiar with your circumstances. However, you may be surprised how much information you absorb from reading these stories.

Acknowledgements

I have always been a story-teller. I tell stories to my wife and friends, my children and their friends. I try to have a moral to the stories so that I don't sound too preachy. I have learned many things from my clients over the years. I feel honored to pass these lessons on to readers who want to take the time to review this book. Most everything I know is contained somewhere in these pages.

The one individual, above all others, I can credit for continued support, is my good friend and co-host of my weekly radio show, Don Parker. He guided me through the process of putting these stories into writing. Don, thank you for all of your support. You are one of the finest men I have ever met. I feel honored to call you a good friend.

I dedicate this book to my father, Charles W. Fisher. He has been my sounding board and I thank him for all of his wisdom and steadfast guidance.

CHARLES W. FISHER

April 27, 1933 – March 3, 2005

Introduction

Over the past twelve years, I have prepared more than three thousand Trusts and another three to five hundred Wills. In addition to all the contacts I've made doing this legal work and document preparation, I have probably met ten to fifteen thousand other people. As a lecturer to Rotary and Kiwanis clubs, retirement groups, real estate groups, charitable groups, church groups, and any other group offering me an invitation, I have spoken to more than twenty thousand people about estate planning issues. I also teach two estate planning classes at the local colleges. In the course of meeting and speaking with all of these people, I have begun to recognize certain patterns — about the type of people who need my services, the way they make and spend their money, how they raise their kids, how they think, and what they want.

This book takes you into my office, and lets you hear their stories. This is my average client: a man (or a married man and wife) between fifty-five to seventy-five years old, with an estate valued between five hundred thousand and one million dollars. Most of my clients are in a long-term marriage (whether their first or second), often over fifty years, and usually have two or three kids. Typically, they have neither received an inheritance, nor had significant financial help from their parents. Most did not have highly-paid jobs, yet with perseverance, patience, and modest skill, have seen their investments grow to a level most never dreamed they'd reach. For some, the money and property — their estate — has become a burden. They have to decide who gets what, in what proportions, and when, and they don't want the government to get any more of their money than necessary. They are conservative and Republican, with only two or three ever admitting to being Democrats.

The men are generally two to four years older than their wives. The women were typically stay-at-home wives, although this is beginning to change (the younger the couple, the more likely the woman held an outside job). Although the households are generally male dominated, the men's abilities sometimes decline due to Alzheimer's or dementia, and their wives find themselves assuming the dominant role. Most of my clients are college educated, but not all of their kids go to college. The men are now retired, but still stay active playing golf, fishing, or playing the stock market. In fact, most clients are amazed at how busy they are and wonder how they ever managed to get anything done when they were working.

They are frugal spenders — clipping coupons from the paper and demanding their ten percent senior citizen discount for a fifty-nine cent cup of coffee. Most have never been involved in a major car accident or been sued. They want to leave their assets to their children, and don't want to be a financial burden to them. Most are religious people. It seems that a strong faith, success, and happiness often go together. Care to meet them? Just step into my office.

Stories

I've had six husbands. I'm still looking for a good one

My client, a lovely woman in her late seventies, scheduled an appointment for a review of her estate. I asked her the standard questions about her estate and what she wanted to do with her assets after her death. She had a son and a daughter and wanted the assets split between the two after her death. We talked about a Living Revocable Trust to avoid probate and I finally asked her about the size of her estate. She was very vague on that point and then she dropped the bombshell.

"I'm not sure how much my estate is worth because I've been married six times. Two of my husbands died and the rest, well, we just parted ways."

I think she noticed the look of disbelief on my face because she said, "I love men. I like being around them but I found that, after a while, I get tired of them."

I said, "I assume you accumulated a little bit from each husband."

She smiled and replied, "Certainly from my two husbands who predeceased me. The last two husbands didn't have much money. In fact, I had a lot more than they did."

"Then you had a premarital agreement?"

She shook her head, "No, I'm not sure what that is, but we didn't sign any papers before we got married."

I was mildly shocked, "You've never had a premarital agreement?"

"No," she responded with a questioning look, "What is that?"

I explained, "A premarital agreement or pre-nuptial agreement is a legal agreement where you and the intended spouse agree that your assets are yours and his assets are his. That way if you ever get divorced, you can't get his assets and more importantly, he can't get yours."

She looked thoughtful and said, “That sounds like an important document I need to have. Could you get one drafted for me?”

“I can get the basic information from you now if you like,” I offered.

She said, “Yes, I'd like that.”

I started with the general questions and then I got to the part about the intended spouse. I said, “Who is the lucky guy?”

“Oh,” she said, “leave that part blank. I've got my eye on several!”

Most busy people don't think about estate planning—other than a simple Will—until one of two events occurs. The first is retirement; the second the death of a family member or close friend.

Disappearing act

The day was progressing smoothly. My next client looked like a banker or an insurance salesman. He was a handsomely dressed gentleman, wearing an expensive silk suit and tie. With his gold rimmed glasses and Rolex watch he had a very self-assured manner about him.

He sat down in my office and said, "I want you to tell me everything you know about Living Revocable Trusts and Durable Powers of Attorney."

I laughed. "Those are two very complex subjects. It could take me several hours to tell you all I know. That would be a pretty expensive lecture, but I'm game if you are."

He put up a hand, "You're right. See if you can narrow it down and tell me how these documents can help my family if I disappear."

I wasn't sure I understood him. "You mean what happens if you fall off a boat and can't be found?"

He shook his head. "Well, no, not exactly."

I tried another tack. "Are you planning on leaving your family?"

"No, not really."

I was beginning to get frustrated. "Then what do you mean by disappear?"

He thought a minute and said, "The Rapture."

"You mean like in the Bible?"

He nodded. "What if I'm taken and my family isn't?"

"Well, I hope I'm not here either," I said, "but, if you disappear and your family is left behind, your Power of Attorney will work until you are declared dead. Likewise, your Living Revocable Trust will provide your family a way to manage your affairs and avoid probate. There's not much else you can do to provide them with more protection, other than buying additional life insurance. I'm pretty sure those companies will still be around after the rapture!"

Legal Analysis: *The Durable Power of Attorney allows you to designate another to make the same financial decisions you can make. The Power of Attorney can be exercised (used) the second after you sign the document. You don't need to be incompetent or unavailable. The document works immediately after signing with no triggering event such as incompetency or unavailability. Likewise, the joint Living Revocable Trust allows either spouse to handle financial affairs without the other's presence, however, unlike the Power of Attorney which stops working at death, the Living Revocable Trust continues to operate after the death of the creator.*

In Florida, a person is declared legally dead if a reasonable explanation of the disappearance can be provided, even if the body can't be found (for example, falling off a cruise liner in the Atlantic with many witnesses.) If a reasonable explanation cannot be provided, then there is a waiting period of five years. After the expiration of that time, the spouse or other interested party can apply for a death certificate.

I was his best wife

A middle-aged woman sat in my office and smiled. She was dressed in what appeared to be the latest New York-style pants suit outfit, with a Gucci handbag and matching shoes.

She began, "I don't really have any problems, I just want to get your advice. Also, I think I may need a Trust for my assets."

"Okay, tell me why you think you need a Trust."

"I've been married several times. My second husband and I got divorced 12 years ago. He had his children and I had mine, but we just couldn't make a go of it. It was kind of a mutual thing. After the divorce, I saw him on a regular basis—nothing sexual."

She smiled, and continued. "We just saw each other and said 'hi,' or had lunch. I kept up with him and he kept up with me. Sometimes we talked about his new wives. I was like his confidant. Since we were married, he could tell me anything."

I nodded. "That must have been strange, since you shared such a close relationship with him."

"Not really. We were just good friends then. Anyway, he got married twice since our divorce. I told him he shouldn't marry the third wife—she was a real bitch. But he didn't listen to me. They lasted about six months. I approved of his last wife. In fact, I encouraged him to marry her. She is a real sweetie. I think he was pretty happy with her."

I looked at her, waiting for more. After a long pause I said, "So what's the problem?"

"His new wife is really nice. I kind of feel a little guilty. He left me the $250,000 in insurance money, and left her with almost nothing."

"Oh my gosh," I mumbled with surprise. "He didn't change the beneficiary designations on his insurance policy?"

"No. He never changed it to his third and fourth wives. The insurance company has already sent me the money and I've spent some of it. There isn't going to be a problem, is there?"

"I don't think so. You were the designated beneficiary of the life insurance policy. You got the check. It's your money."

She hesitantly probed, "So she has no claim to it?"

I responded, "No, it's all yours. Do you think he meant for all of the money to go to you?"

"We've been divorced for 12 years. He remarried twice. I think he forgot." Then I saw a certain resolve in her eyes. She wasn't taking any chances. "However, we did maintain a close relationship. I presume if he wanted his new wife to get this insurance money, he would have changed his insurance beneficiary. Besides, I was his best wife."

Legal Analysis: *If your Will named your former wife as the sole beneficiary, she is instantly removed, by law, the moment the final divorce papers are signed. The Will can be read as though your wife predeceased you. The beneficiaries that would inherit if she predeceased you will then inherit. This is not the case for the beneficiary designation on insurance and all other financial documents. Those designations override any beneficiary designation on your Will or Trust. If your IRA or life insurance beneficiary is your former wife or old girl friend, she gets the money, regardless of what your Will says.*

Pass the olive oil

Sometimes you get a second chance to correct mistakes. In this case the dad, my client, established a Living Revocable Trust and named his eldest son, John, as the Successor Trustee of the Trust as well as his Power of Attorney. Dad's un-medicated, bi-polar daughter, Jane, was living with him at the time he created the Trust. He was supporting her financially and she was helping with the housework. He paid for office space so she could have a job and a place to go during the day. Dad knew she had some mental issues, but they were not debilitating and he was able to maintain control over her with the checkbook.

The first time I met him he came to my office, accompanied by Jane. She attended all the meetings. After naming his son, John, in all positions of financial authority, Dad turned to Jane and said, "Honey, you can be my Health Care Surrogate, which means you'll make health care decisions for me if I am unable to make them myself." She was pleased that she was included and I'm sure Dad thought that since Jane wasn't in control of the money, there would be no harm in making her his health care surrogate. I didn't know she had mental problems or I would have suggested an alternate choice.

About a year later, Dad suffered a serious heart attack and was hospitalized for more than a month. With her dad in a coma, Jane, as health care surrogate, was in charge of all healthcare decisions, exercising her rights under the Health Care Surrogate document Dad had signed. As time went by, there were small disagreements among the other children regarding the decisions made for Dad's care and treatment. Unfortunately, the longer Dad remained in the hospital, the more control Jane exerted and her behavior became increasingly erratic. Eventually, she started to limit visitation for her brothers and sisters, telling them Dad needed his rest or that it wasn't a good time to visit. Her siblings were very upset with this behavior, but there was little they could do—Jane was now firmly in control of Dad's doctors and all healthcare decisions. During this time, Dad was just barely clinging to life and emotions were running high. Jane's behavior was becoming more and more disruptive. She was rude to the hospital staff and even pushed a nurse.

While riding her wave of new found power, Jane told brother John that she wanted to remodel the house for Dad's convalescent care. She wanted new carpeting and new appliances. Although Dad had money, he was tighter than bark to a tree. He drove a 1975 pick-up truck with no air conditioning. "Purrs like a kitten," he would say. His household furnishings were purchased in 1957 — "They look fine." His appliances came with the house when purchased in 1962. He bought his first microwave oven just three years ago but was still using the toaster he and his wife got as a wedding present in 1954. "If it ain't broke, why replace it?" John fumed that any money spent on remodeling the house and purchasing new furnishings would cause Dad's blood pressure to erupt like Mount St. Helens.

Meanwhile, back at the hospital, his bi-polar daughter was running the show and had slowly evolved from the helping daughter to the "woman in charge." She finally had the position of authority in the family she always coveted, and was in total control of Dad's life. The rest of the family was outraged and could only wonder what Dad was thinking when he selected Jane as the Health Care Surrogate.

After these incidents, John called me and scheduled a meeting. At the meeting, he looked at me with puzzled eyes and said, "You did Dad's Trust. What was he thinking when he selected Jane as the Health Care Surrogate?"

I reeled back, and said, "I don't know. I asked who he wanted for that position and he gave me her name. I didn't ask if she had mental problems."

"Do you have any idea what she is doing to our Dad?" he questioned.

I shook my head, "No."

He put his hands on his head and rolled his eyes and said, "Late at night, she stays in his room, and she rubs his entire body down with olive oil. She says it helps his skin from drying out."

I gasped, "The whole body?"

"Yeah, it's pretty sick," he retorted. Then he looked at me and said,

"I sure hope Dad gets better so I can kick his ass for all the trouble he's caused me and the rest of the family. I really want to cuss him out." He had tears in his eyes as he said this.

After another week, Dad's condition improved to the point he was able to sit up and make his own decisions. As soon as he could talk, the family and hospital staff were able to ignore Jane (the nurse-pushing incident had caused her to be banned from the hospital). I was summoned to prepare a new Health Care Surrogate document naming John as the surrogate in charge. With a great sigh of relief, John accepted the document after Dad signed it.

I asked Dad why he had selected his mentally unstable daughter instead of his son, who was clearly more responsible.

"She was living with me at the time and I didn't want to hurt her feelings," he said sheepishly.

"That's not a good reason," I said.

"You're right, but I've learned my lesson. I can't believe some of the things she did to me."

Then he winked and rubbed his arm, "But I have to admit, my skin sure feels soft."

Legal Analysis: *The Health Care Surrogate document allows the designated person to control all heath care decisions. This person has priority even over a spouse. This power only springs into action when the maker is no longer able to indicate their direction. A wink or a nod can indicate your directions. In contrast, a Durable Power of Attorney for financial decisions is legally effective the moment it is signed. The named power of attorney can use it immediately and it does not require a triggering event, such as incapacity or unavailability.*

The last gasp

In a recent case of mine, an elderly couple was traveling in their car. A hurricane had just passed through Pensacola, Florida, and this was their first trip away from their home. The power was still out at their home and they were out shopping for supplies. While traveling cautiously down the road, they approached a non-functioning traffic light at a major intersection. An Alabama man, with a big car and trailering a big boat, was also approaching the intersection from another direction. The elderly couple passed through the intersection an instant before the Alabama man, precipitating a classic T-bone crash. The impact was horrific, scattering parts of the couple's car for hundreds of yards. A few minutes after the accident, a police officer arrived on the scene. He found the elderly couple's twisted and broken bodies and heard the wife groan, but when he reached her in the wreckage she was dead. Her husband, lying next to her, was also dead. The officer reported the husband died at 12:00 p.m. and the wife at 12:01 p.m. The times of death and the order of death were clearly evident and the couple had no children and no Wills. Florida Statutes dictate that since the wife clearly survived her husband, if only by one minute, the wife's family received all the estate assets.

Legal Analysis: *All recent Florida Wills—including the ones I draft—have a common death clause. This means that if the death of both spouses occurs at or near the same time, the estate assets shall be distributed according to the directions in the Will. Both Wills say the same thing, so under the law the outcome is cast in stone. There is also a survivorship clause most lawyers insert in Wills and Trusts. This clause says that in order to inherit, the beneficiary must survive the decedent by 30, 60 or 90 days. This means that one must outlive the decedent by the specified time. Without the time limitations, if a beneficiary outlived the decedent by five minutes, then the beneficiary's Will would control where the estate assets would go. With the survivorship clause, the decedent's Will or Trust would always control in the case of common deaths or deaths occurring at or near the same time.*

Who owns my house?

The woman was clearly worried, looking at me expectantly, as if I would be the one to solve all her problems.

So I asked her, “You look as though you have some questions?”

She nodded. “I want to know what has happened to my assets.”

She pushed a pile of estate documents across the table and said, “I lost the homestead exemption on my house. Also, my broker just told me I couldn’t access my account.”

That did sound serious. “Let me look over your papers and see if I can figure out what’s going on.” I offered, and started my review of the documents as she sat in her chair twitching. After a few more minutes had passed, she started talking and told me the story.

She said her mother had a Trust prepared by a very fine local law firm at some considerable expense. She figured if the Trust was good enough for her mother it should be good enough for her as well. So wanting to save a few bucks she copied her mother’s Trust, word for word. Every place her mother’s name appeared, she inserted her name. In those places where her own name appeared, she substituted the names of her three children. She signed the Trust agreement and her children signed it as well.

It didn’t take me long to determine this particular Trust had been set up to provide the mother with certain protections for Medicaid planning. To that end, the mother had given all of her assets to her daughter, (my client) as Trustee, to control. When my client copied and signed the Trust she gave all of her assets to her three children. The house was in the children’s name, as Trustees. As a result, she lost her homestead exemption because her name was not on the deed as Trustee. When she called her broker he told her she did not have access to her account because it was now owned by her children—as Trustees—and her name was not on the account.

“I hope you have a great relationship with your children, because they own all of your assets and are not legally required to give them back,” I said.

“I THINK I have a great relationship. We’ll soon find out, won’t we?”

This is one of the best examples I have ever seen for not being your own lawyer and doing your own legal work. If you don't know what you're doing, copying someone else's Trust document can be risky. There are so many potential legal pitfalls in estate work. How can you be sure you have done everything right if you don't know what you're doing?

Occasionally, I'll meet with a do-it-yourselfer who gets cold feet. They may have spent a lot of time and even some money putting together their own Trust, but eventually they start having doubts. I remember one retired executive who told me "I've done my own Trust, but I just don't have confidence in my work. Will you prepare a Trust package for my wife and me so I can stop worrying?"

Legal Analysis: *Copying someone else's documents may not be the right thing for you and your family. Once the document is executed, it is a binding legal document. Much thought and legal analysis goes into to each and every estate plan. A layperson may think estate plans such as Trusts and Wills are all the same, but they aren't. Most lawyers don't draft a 100-page Trust package including a Will, Durable Power of Attorney, Living Will, and Health Care Surrogate from scratch. They have certain formats they use. Some Trusts include language regarding the level of control a Trustee or co-Trustee can exercise. Some Trusts deal with married couples; some with singles. Some include children and grandchildren. I have drafted over two thousand Trusts and met with 12 thousand to 15 thousand people. I can generally get a good idea about what a person or couple needs in the first thirty minutes. The rest of the time is spent fine-tuning the Trust documents to fit their particular needs. To the layperson, decisions about what should be done may appear to be made quickly, but they are usually based on years of experience. Many of the do-it-yourself Wills end up in litigation or in court with flaws costing the heirs many times the expense of paying a lawyer a fee to set it up right the first time.*

Where's the shotgun?

An elderly gentleman in his seventies explained his estate situation to me. He had approximately three million dollars in assets that he and his wife had accumulated during their fifty years of marriage. He had lost his wife two years earlier and had not remarried, but his three grown children were all doing well.

After going over some additional details I said, "Your estate seems pretty straight forward. I assume you want to avoid estate taxes and leave your assets to your three children?"

Surprisingly he shook his head. "No, just the opposite. I don't want to leave my children any of my estate."

"You mean you don't want to pay any estate taxes?"

He shook his head again. "I'm telling you, I don't want to leave any of my estate to my children."

I was puzzled. "Well, it's your money and your estate; you can certainly do with it as you please. But why would you leave your children nothing? I could understand if they were bums or deadbeats, but you said they were decent children."

"Yes, they certainly are," he said, "and that's the point. I don't want to spoil them with a lot of money. My wife and I had nothing when we got married. We never got a dime from anyone. We worked hard and believe me we suffered at times. We made our own luck and ultimately we were very successful. I don't want to deprive my children of the same life we had, and I truly believe that giving them too much money will deprive them of that opportunity."

While I understood his point, I still had a mental vision of his children stalking into my office carrying shotguns and demanding to know why I had allowed their father to cut them out of his Will. With that image in my mind, I discussed different ways to keep the children in as beneficiaries. Each time I would suggest something, he would say "No."

After about an hour, I was about to give up. Then I suddenly had an idea. "Why don't you tie the children's inheritance to their work performance?"

"What do you mean?"

"Leave your assets in Trust managed by a Trust company you select," I said. "The children would then present their tax returns each year and their gross income would be matched by the Trustee."

He liked this idea. We made some minor modifications and finally he signed a Trust document which would hold his assets in Trust and allow each child to present their 1040 tax return each year to claim a share of the Trust assets. He felt this would be sufficient motivation for each child to continue to be successful. The more money they made, the more money they'd get from the Trust. There were some obvious problems with the plan, such as encouraging the children to not be tax efficient, but they weren't overwhelming. As far as I was concerned, the important thing was that the children were back in the Will and I wouldn't be looking down the barrels of any shotguns.

He was satisfied with my solution and I documented my file so I could explain to his children what we did and how close they came to getting nothing.

Legal Analysis: *There is no law requiring one to leave assets to a child, and no explanation is required if a child is left out of a Will. A sentence in a Will or Trust saying, "I acknowledge I have a son, John, and direct he receive nothing from my Will," is sufficient to eliminate him. It's your money and your assets and you can dispose of them in any way you desire. You can give it to the children all at once, over time, or not at all.*

Home Depot got my money

The husband and wife were sitting in my office and the wife said, "Our daughter is not very responsible and will immediately give her husband any money we bequeath her. Her husband is nice enough, but he has a problem handling money."

I said I understood, and asked what they wanted to do with their estate after their deaths.

Mom announced, "We'd like it tied up so she can't get any of it until she's sixty-two years old."

Dad was in full agreement. "No money until she's sixty-two," he said.

This is when I really like my job. I get to ask the nosey questions and find out the real story. Parents are brutally honest with their doctors and their lawyers, and I often find out what parents really think about their children. I believe the true nature of a child is determined at birth. Parents see and recognize these personality traits at a young age and these traits don't change much as the child grows older.

"My daughter is a lovely person, a great mom and wife, but she's just not strong emotionally." Mom said. "We've given her eleven thousand dollars on two separate occasions, but she just gave the check to her husband."

"He cashed the check and took all of the cash to Home Depot," Dad grumbled, "and bought yard equipment, a tractor, and a bunch of other useless stuff. He spent the entire damn amount in one day and he did it again when we gave her the second check." He shook his head. "How could anyone spend all that money in one day?"

As he said this, I was thinking about the wood-working tools, cabinets, toilets, faucets, and the new lawn tractor I would have bought with that money. I suddenly realized they were waiting for me to say something. "There's no doubt about it," I agreed, "your son-in-law is out of control, but I think I can help."

After another hour of discussion, Mom and Dad came to an agreement. They would establish A/B Living Revocable Trusts directing the

Trustee, at the last death, to hold all of their daughter's assets in Trust until she reached the age of sixty-two years. Dad said, "Even if she gives all of our estate to her husband at least she'll still get her social security."

I pointed out that their estate was so large it was still advisable to gift this $11,000 amount to their daughter. "If you don't give it to her now, the IRS will get almost fifty percent of it when you die."

"I don't give a damn," Dad said. "I'd rather the IRS get my money than that bum."

Mom winked at me. "And you never know. If he realizes he can't get any of her money, maybe he'll dump her."

Legal Analysis: *No law requires that you leave your estate assets to your children at a particular time. This couple could have omitted her completely if they desired. They can certainly control the timing and amount of the distributions. I have prepared many estate plans where the distributions to children occur later in life, such as ages 55 to 65. I have worked on many distributions where the child never gets the principal of the estate. The principal is held in Trust and the child receives income but not the principal. Some parents feel a large influx of cash will spoil a child. Others feel their children are irresponsible with money and want to protect them against themselves. Still others know that any large inheritance, more than a couple thousand dollars, could possibly cause the death of their child, who would use the money for alcohol or drugs. If this is the case, the parents want their child to receive a small monthly stipend that will allow the child to pay for a small apartment, food, and little else. If they use the money for drugs or alcohol, they will not have a place to sleep. After a few nights sleeping in the woods, the child may use the next check to pay for rent. The child can count on receiving a monthly check to pay for some of the necessities. If the amount came in a lump sum, it would be gone within a short time leaving the child without that lifetime financial security blanket.*

Honey, the Sheriff wants you

My clients were sitting across the table from me looking nervous and anxious. They both looked sleep-deprived with heavy lids and dark rings under their eyes. The husband slid some papers across the table. His wife turned her head as her eyes welled up with tears.

"We got this two days ago," he said. "We tried to get an appointment with you yesterday, but you were booked solid."

I picked up the papers. It was a summons and complaint. I reviewed the complaint and attachments. My clients were being sued for $1.5 million dollars. I looked at them and said, "Tell me what happened."

The wife said, "It all started when my father died eight years ago. I am an only child. He didn't have a very big estate, just a house, some investments, and a small gas station convenience store, like a 7-11. We got a buyer for the store but to make a quick sale, our lawyer had me move the ownership of the store from my father's estate to our name, which allowed us to sell right away instead of waiting for the estate to close. At least that is what he told me. Anyway, we owned the store and property for two months before the sale. On the day of closing, some environmental guy went by and took a soil sample near one of the buried gas tanks. He called and stopped the closing because he said there was a leak in the tank and gasoline was leaking into the ground. The buyer hired an environmental engineering firm to fix the tank and remove the contaminated soil and we adjusted the sale price to pay for these expenses. After 6 weeks, the job was completed and the closing went on as scheduled. I got a check and that was the last I heard of the buyer or the store, until two days ago, when a deputy sheriff showed up at my house."

I reviewed the papers and said, "From what I can see, it looks as though your buyer sold the store to a new buyer, but the soil did not pass the new EPA standards. They are estimating it will cost about $1.5 million to clean up the mess. The Super Fund has paid to clean up the contaminated soil and now it is seeking reimbursement from all owners that fall within the chain of title. Since your names appear on record as title-owners, you become personally liable."

"But we only owned the store for a little over two months!"

I nodded. "I understand. However, it doesn't make any difference how long you owned the property. Owning it for one day places you in the chain of title and therefore legally responsible."

"What does this mean for us?"

"Well," I said, "It means you are personally liable for all or part of the $1.5 million dollar clean-up bill."

"Oh my God. Can they take our house? Are we going to lose everything?"

"In Florida, your house is protected by Homestead Law and can't be taken by a creditor. Your home can only be taken by the mortgage company foreclosing on the mortgage, the IRS, a domestic order, or through a mechanic's lien. All of your IRA's and qualified annuities are also protected from creditors."

She said, "That's a comfort. At least I can sleep tonight knowing we won't lose the house and the retirement accounts. That's the bulk of our estate assets anyway."

Legal Analysis: *If your name appears in the chain of title for real property (real estate), then you may have personal liability exposure. In the case above, I would have advised against dropping the convenience store property out of the estate into the daughter's name. I would have recommended that the property be sold as an estate asset thereby eliminating the daughter from personal liability exposure. The environmental laws are so severe that this type of planning should be considered before any real property is taken into an individual name. If there is any doubt, the title could be taken in the name of a corporation or a Limited Liability Company to avoid personal exposure.*

Epilog: *As of this writing, my client is still in litigation with the EPA.*

Tale of two sisters

After discussing his estate plan and making the necessary decisions, the client asked, “Are you familiar with Medicaid and nursing home issues?”

“Yes, I do a fair amount of Medicaid planning for clients.”

“I want to tell you a true tale about my mother and her sister.”

“Okay,” I said.

He started by saying, “My grandmother died when my mother and aunt were young. My grandfather raised his two daughters by himself. They both had nothing but fond memories growing up. Apparently, he was a very good dad. Anyway, he finally passed away at age 89. My mother was 70 and my aunt was 69. He left each of them an inheritance of about $100,000.” I interrupted and asked, “What year did he die?” He responded, “He died in 1987. After the estate taxes were paid, my mother and my aunt each ended up with about $100,000. My aunt never had any children and has always been somewhat of a free spirit. My mother, however, has always been very conservative and frugal. My aunt took her inheritance and traveled the world. There was little she didn’t do. I think she went to Europe several times. My mother relayed the fantastic exploits of my aunts’ travels. My mother, on the other hand, kept her money and tried to save it. She did a pretty good job keeping the principal intact over the years. She took the interest to supplement her social security.”

I interjected, “I’m getting the picture that your aunt was the wandering sole who spent every dime she got and your mother saved and scrimped to provide for her future.”

“Exactly,” he exclaimed, “You’re right. My aunt had a good time and squandered all of her inheritance. My mother saved her money and sacrificed her lifestyle because she was providing for the future.”

“What happened?”

He finished, “Not long ago, my aunt needed a nursing home. Since she was destitute by that time, she qualified for Medicaid. She had no problem finding a free Medicaid room in a nursing home. I was a little concerned for her at the time. My concern must have been apparent on my face. I vividly remember my aunt looking at me and saying, 'I always knew when one door closed, another one would open.' My mother needed a nursing home about a year later. We got her into the same nursing home where my aunt was staying. Because my mother still had the $100,000 inheritance left, she had to pay the nursing home bills until her money was completely exhausted. Of course, it's now all gone. My mother and aunt are in the same nursing home just down the hall from each other. The only difference is my mother had to spend all of her inheritance to pay for the nursing home and my aunt did not. Somehow it just doesn't seem fair. The system penalizes the savers—the ones who try to provide for their future. It rewards those who squander their money and make no provisions for the future."

I said, "You're right. It's not fair. I'm not sure, though, how to make it fair. The bottom line for you personally is that your mother is being taken care of, and you don't have to pay the nursing home bill yourself. Those who can't afford to pay will have a place to stay. Regardless of the financial status, no one will be left on the street."

Legal Analysis: *<u>Medicaid asset qualifying rules for a single person</u>: One homestead of any value; one engagement ring and one wedding ring of any value; one car; approximately $2500 in burial related funds; $2000 in other assets, like checking and savings.*

<u>Medicaid asset qualifying rules for married couple</u>: One home of any value. Approximately $96,000 of other assets are excluded.

The Medicaid rules are very complicated and ever changing. When a gap or loophole appears and people take advantage of it, the Department issues new rules to correct the perceived wrong. The basic idea of providing nursing care services for those in need and who can't afford it is sound. It's just that some of the inequities are quite severe. For example, consider two married couples each with a net worth of $290,000. One couple has a house worth $200,000. The other couple has moved out of their house to provide more liquidity and cash. They are living in an apartment. Their assets of $290,000 are invested in interest bear-

ing accounts like CD's and bonds. Each couple has the same size estate. The first couple can qualify for Medicaid nursing home benefits immediately. Their $200,000 home is excluded from Medicaid consideration. The remaining $90,000 cash is excluded under the Medicaid rules. The second couple can exclude $90,000 in cash but the remaining $200,000 is not excluded. It must be "spent down" before the second couple can qualify for Medicaid. In other words, the second couple must pay for their own monthly nursing care bills ($4000 to $8000 per month) until their nest egg is gone. The first couple keeps all of their assets but the second couple does not.

These rules will change over time and are even quite different now state to state. There may be quite a bit of state Medicaid shopping in the future, if one state has more favorable rules than another state. Check with your local Medicaid office or an Elder Care Attorney for the qualifying rules in your state.

Parents are brutally honest with their doctors and their lawyers, and I often find out what parents really think about their children. I believe the true nature of a child is determined at birth. Parents see and recognize these personality traits at a young age and those traits don't change much as the child grows.

Are we done yet?

An elderly couple sitting in my client chairs discussed their estate assets. Each contributed to the conversation about what they had and where they wanted their assets to go after they were gone. The gentleman was quite brilliant. He asked pointed and relevant questions and I had no trouble communicating with him. After a while, the discussion dragged on a bit as we rehashed the same issues and I noticed the wife starting to dominate the conversation. She was asking the same questions over and over again. The gentleman looked at me and, without interrupting his wife, quietly asked me if I had all of the information I needed. The wife was still talking, but I said that I did. As the wife continued to talk, he removed both hearing aids, placed them in his pocket, and sat back in his chair with a contented look on his face. His wife talked for another thirty minutes, but he never said another word, except "So long" when they left. This gentleman definitely understands the old something about keeping the peace in his home or maybe, he understands the old saying, "silence is golden."

Knock, knock. I've come to live with you again.

Life has many twists and turns. Certain events are expected: trouble with jobs, a spouse, finances, and the kids. However, most people grow up and move out of the house, never imagining that they might one day have trouble with a parent. After you left the nest, you expected your parents would be there to take you back if circumstances required you to return home. But as you make your own life in your own house with your own family, you have to face your own problems every day. You cope with the daily issues and deal with juggling schedules for work, car pools, and school activities for the kids, in addition to your spouses' needs. You have to deal with all the usual aggravations of life and certainly don't need any more stress.

Let's assume your mother has passed away, and your elderly father lives by himself in West Texas. One night around 10 P.M. there comes a knock at the door. You open it and find your father standing there. He tells you he has driven all the way from Texas. He says "I can't stay in my house alone any more. I left before the state division of family services had me committed. You see, I caught my stove on fire last week. There was an investigation and they said I wasn't really able to take care of myself." He tells you he's having trouble remembering things and asks if he can stay with you for a while.

Still trying to absorb this news, you're stunned by his request—the thought never entered your mind. You already have the responsibility of taking care of a job, a husband, two kids, a dog, a cat and five salt-water aquarium fish. Now, like a bolt of lightening, your father has appeared and your life will never be the same.

Think back to the time before marriage and kids. You were free. You came and went as you pleased. Then someone came into your life and you got married. It took a while to settle down and get used to having someone under foot. You had to learn to adjust and be considerate. After a while of living with your new husband, life became free and fun again. It was the two of you. You were living together and you could do whatever you wanted. It was great. Then you got pregnant. Life changed again. More adjustments to your lifestyle and accommodations were made. Then another child came, and another. After many years of adjusting, you finally start to see the light at the end of the tunnel. The kids will leave the nest in a couple of years. The dog, cat, and the fish will all be dead by then and it will just be you and your husband. You can be together again. You can travel and do some of the things you have put off because of kids, time, and money.

Now your Dad is here. What do you do? Where will he stay? How are you going to manage all of the things you have going on in your life and now take care of Dad? The issues are endless. You need legal control if he continues his mental decline. A Power of Attorney, Health Care Surrogate, Living Will, Will, and Living Revocable Trust are documents to consider. Brothers and sisters should be consulted. If Dad is mentally incompetent, a formal guardianship must be initiated. What about his income and assets? Should he pay rent? What about nursing home care and who will pay the costs? There's an old Yiddish expression that sums it up very well, "Man plans and God laughs."

Legal Analysis: *This situation can be a can of worms. Taking care of your parent may, in some respects, be more difficult than taking care of your own children. If a parent has sufficient assets, the burden is less. However, if they exhibit destructive behavior because of declining mental abilities, you can have a serious problem. Your other siblings may or may not contribute their money or their time, but you can be assured they will expect to share equally in his estate. My advice is to have a family meeting and let all siblings participate. Some families will not conform to this model and there will be problems. I wouldn't be in business if everyone could amicably resolve their problems. Thank goodness for families that don't plan properly and want to fight over the estate!*

Protect me against myself

Most lawyers don't seek legal advice from other lawyers. Why pay for something you can do yourself? Regrettably, this mindset is the reason most lawyers' estates end up in a messy probate. They just never got around to doing a Will or Trust or finding the time to do the necessary research. If they did one at all, it is usually very basic with no significant estate planning decisions considered.

With this insight, I was impressed to see a very tough litigator in my office. However, at first I was a little uneasy, not knowing the reason for him being in my office.

Then he said, "Mark, I understand you do a lot of Trust work."

Relieved, I said, "That's right, I just do Trusts and probate."

"Good, I want you to create an irrevocable Trust for me. You can do that, can't you?"

"Sure, that's no problem. Are you wanting this irrevocable Trust for inheritance tax protection, or liability protection?"

He replied, "I want it to protect me against myself."

I didn't say a word but my eyes gave away my question. "*What in the hell are you talking about?*"

"I know what you're thinking, but let me tell you. I've been married four times. I really love women. I can't help myself. Unfortunately, I'm a real bastard to live with. When they finally realize this, they want a divorce. My first wife lasted 15 years and we had two children. She finally divorced me and nearly wiped me out financially. I've had three wives since then. They each did pretty well financially when we got divorced. As a result, I don't have much left. The next time I have the urge to get married, I'm just going to go to a bar, find a woman I really don't like, and buy her a house. It would probably be cheaper for me in the end."

"Did you ever consider a pre-marital agreement?" I asked in amazement.

“No, it never seemed like the thing to do. I was always so much in love, I couldn’t imagine getting divorced.”

I said, “Certainly, by the last marriage you noticed a pattern? Divorce left you broke.”

“That’s the problem, I lose my mind. I am so much in love I can’t protect myself and I do stupid things. That’s why I need you to prepare an irrevocable Trust I can never change. I can’t give my assets away and most importantly; a new wife can’t take them from me. My brother has agreed to be my Trustee. He will control my assets and my investments. He knows what’s best for me.”

“What if your brother decides to keep all of your money, and not let you have any?” I asked.

“That’s just a risk I’m prepared to take.”

After several additional meetings and many reviews of the irrevocable Trust document, it was ready to be signed.

I said, “This is the final draft you have already reviewed. Do you want to look at it again?”

“No,” he said. “I’m ready to sign.”

The witnesses were all present and I reviewed the general terms of the document by saying, “You have read this Trust. Do you understand it is non-changeable?”

He responded, “Yes, I understand.”

“Okay,” I said, “Initial each page on the bottom right corner and then sign the last two pages above your type-written name.”

He complied. After the document was passed around the conference table and signed by all necessary witnesses and the notary, I had the document copied.

After it was returned, I stapled all of the pages together and handed the completed original document to him saying, “This is it, your irrevocable Trust. How does it feel not to be in control of your assets?”

“You have no idea how much love I have to spread around,” he said, smiling. “I feel like a liberated man. I have protected my future. I don’t suppose you know of any good looking rich widows who want to share some of my love?” As he strolled out of my office, he winked at my secretary.

Legal Analysis: *The most common use of the irrevocable Trust is for inheritance tax avoidance. If the asset has been moved out of your estate, and you can’t get it back, then neither can the IRS. Much time is spent on the transferring of assets from an estate to an irrevocable Trust to keep the assets from being taxed after death. There are many types of non- changeable Trusts, but the most common is the Irrevocable Life Insurance Trust (ILIT). This Trust holds a life insurance policy. If properly established, the ILIT keeps the life insurance death benefits out of the estate and thus not taxed by the IRS.*

The second most common irrevocable Trust is for asset protection. If your assets are tied up so that you can’t get them, then neither can a creditor. The single most important issue in this situation is for the Trust to be established before you knew or should have known of the liability. If you’ve been in a serious car accident, and it’s your fault, it’s generally too late to set up an irrevocable Trust to protect your assets.

We got some estate planning tips from a "friend"

A very nice retired couple moved to the Florida panhandle. They purchased a lovely waterfront home on Santa Rosa Sound, an inland waterway. Wanting to do some estate planning for inheritance taxes, they added their grandchildren to their deed when they purchased the property. Several years later, two back-to-back hurricanes devastated their waterfront property. The dock and seawall were both destroyed, rebuilt, and destroyed again, all within two months.

Tired of evacuating their home and worrying about the destructive force of the hurricanes, they found a nice home on a nearby golf course. They contacted me to help with the sale of their waterfront property and the purchase of their new golf course property. Upon reviewing their deed, I noticed something odd. I saw two other owners of their property identified on their deed.

My clients were sitting across the conference table from me when I looked up and said, "Who are these people on the deed with you?"

The wife smiled and said, "Oh, they're our grandchildren. We added them to the deed when we purchased the home five years ago. A friend of ours said it would save on inheritance taxes later."

I felt a sinking sensation in the pit of my stomach. "How old are your grandchildren?" I asked.

She said, "One is nine and the other fourteen." They told me the "friend" explained that if the grandchildren owned the property with them, any increase in the value of the property would occur in the estates of the grandchildren, since each now owned 25%. If the waterfront property had a value of $400,000, then only $200,000 would be in the name of my clients because each grandchild owned 25% or $100,000. At the death of my clients, only 50% of the value of the land would be included in their estate for estate tax consideration.

The sinking sensation I was experiencing grew stronger. Under Florida Law (and the laws in every other state) minors cannot control real property. This must be done through a guardian and a formal legal procedure.

I said, "I hope you have a great relationship with your grandchildren and their parents because you can't sell your home unless each grandchild signs the deed. Unfortunately, your grandchildren are minors and can't legally sign for themselves and their parents can't sign for them either. A separate legal guardian for each grandchild must be appointed to sign the deed."

They gave me a bewildered look. "What does this mean?" they asked.

I sighed and explained, "It means you can't sell your house unless a guardianship is established for each grandchild. You'll have to hire a lawyer to establish two separate guardianships and there must be a separate legal procedure for each grandchild. It will cost a couple thousand dollars, just in legal fees, to establish the guardianship to sell your house. And it doesn't end there. The sale of the house must be approved by the guardian and must be in the best interest of your grandchildren. If your house is approved for sale and ultimately sold, your decision to use the proceeds to purchase a new house will be evaluated. The guardians will determine if the new home you are seeking to purchase is in the best interest of the wards (the grandchildren). In your case, the new prospective home is several hundred thousand dollars less expensive than the waterfront property, which means the extra proceeds will need to be invested in restricted accounts approved by the guardians."

When I finished, my clients didn't know what to do. They left without doing anything. They still live in their waterfront home, waiting for the children to reach the age of eighteen, hoping they turn out to be mature, responsive, and cooperative grandchildren. Luckily, the recent hurricanes have been fairly mild.

Legal Analysis: *There were other issues affecting my clients that we didn't get a chance to discuss in detail. I figured they had heard enough bad news for one afternoon. They were stuck unless they initiated the guardianship. Routinely, people add a child or* *grandchild to their home deed or to other property with the best of intentions. But the problems created by this act, including the above problem, can be significant. Adding the two grandchildren to the deed caused this couple to unwittingly give up the greatest asset protection tool available in Florida, their homestead.*

In Florida, the homestead is the financial fortress. Only the mortgage company, the IRS, and a repairman (using a mechanic's lien) can take the home. No creditor can file a judgment or lien against the home. However, after the grandchild is added, this protection is lost. When the grandchild reaches the age of 18 years he can move in—it's his house too. He can rent out a room if he wants and creditors can force the sale of the house to satisfy his debts. That same grandchild could also force the sale of the house on the courthouse steps, using a legal partition action, and have the house sold to collect his 25% interest in cash. Of course, most grandchildren are nice and sweet and would never do anything like this. Unfortunately, nice and sweet grandchildren eventually grow into teenagers and some of those teenagers will have tattoos, tongue bars, and purple hair. They turn eighteen and think they know what's best for them. They may decide that since it's their property, too, they want it, now. It doesn't matter that you gave it to them as a gift. Part of it belongs to them and they can control it whether or not you agree with their decision.

Few lawyers, if any, would have advised this couple to add the grandchildren to the deed as joint owners. Rarely do I ever feel it is appropriate to have property jointly owned by more than one person. Obviously, property ownership between husband and wife is usually proper, but if tax or succession planning is a consideration, then even this form of ownership can cause problems.

There may be times when joint ownership is appropriate. Let's say an eighty-five-year-old widow with only one child, a sixty-year-old daughter, visits me to discuss estate planning. Mom's only assets are a bank account and her newly purchased patio home. The daughter is already a joint owner on Mom's bank checking account, and in this case, I would add the daughter to Mom's deed as a joint owner with "rights of survivorship." If Mom has more than one child, or an older house, it is generally *not a good idea to add the children to Mom's deed. More names added to the deed will just expand the potential liability. Also, if the children are added as property owners, most of the automatic stepped-up tax basis is lost. For instance, if the property was purchased for $25,000 in 1950 and now is worth $175,000, the capital gain would be $150,000 ($175,000 minus the original purchase price of $25,000), so a capital gains tax of $20,000 would be due. If there were two children on the deed, Mom would be a one-third owner and her one-third interest would receive a step-up in basis as the result of her death. The remaining two-thirds interest ($100,000) does not receive the stepped-up basis because the property interest was received as a gift. The $100,000 gain upon sale will be taxed at the children's capital gains tax rate, up to 15% or $15,000. Had Mom left the home in her name, then died, the home could be sold with no capital gain taxes due since all assets receive a stepped-up tax basis after death.*

"Oh, Shit!"

She brought a big pile of papers into my office and plopped them on my desk. She looked at me with a certain anticipation in her eyes. It seemed she wanted to know something.

She said, "I really don't understand all of this estate stuff. These papers show I'm getting an inheritance. The estate is about $3 million. I want you to review these papers and let me know what's happening."

She pushed the pile of papers to my side of the desk. I quickly organized them and started my review. After reviewing and handling hundreds of estates I was familiar with the pleadings and correspondence.

I said, "It appears you are correct. The estate has a value of about $3 million. There are three beneficiaries receiving equal shares, of which you are one. Since the estate value is $3 million, the lawyer representing the estate is preparing a 706 estate tax return. Any estate over $675,000 (now over $1.5 million) is required to file a return and pay inheritance taxes on the amount over $675,000. Barring any unusual problems, I estimate the estate taxes due the IRS to be about $1.2 million.

Her eyes betrayed mild shock. I could see she was mentally dividing the remaining balance by three.

"And," I continued, "the 706 has not yet been filed. The estate has a nine-month window to file the return, and then the IRS reviews it. That entire process takes one to two years, on the average."

There was a pause, then a low gasp. "Oh, shit," is all she said.

"Pardon me?"

"Two years."

"That's right. Do you want me to help you with anything else?"

"No," she said, "You've done enough."

She then got up, collected her papers, and left my office. I looked out the window and watched her drive away in a brand-new Mercedes SUV. The temporary paper tag was still attached to the back window.

Legal Analysis: *The average probate estate takes about 18 months from beginning to completion. If a 706 inheritance tax return is due, the average time is increased to about two years. Most state laws prevent distributions of estate assets for a period of at least five months. (See, for example, F.S. 733.801.) This is because the Personal Representative is personally responsible to pay the debts of the estate. The estate assets are used to pay for these debts, and once the assets are exhausted, the Personal Representative reports to the court that the estate has no more assets to pay debts. The Personal Representative is then released. However, if the Personal Representative made a distribution of assets to the heirs prior to the closing of the estate and then discovered another outstanding debt, the Personal Representative is personally liable for the debt. Once informed of this personal liability, most Personal Representative's understandably wait until the probate process has run its full course before final distributions are made.*

It's amazing how much smarter you think you are when you have a lot of money. It's even more amazing how much smarter others think you are because you have a lot of money even if you didn't do anything to get it other than being born.

What is that flushing sound?

The twists and turns of fate are never ending, and this tale leads to a unique watery grave. It starts with a young man and woman who met, fell in love, and then married. The young sweet wife was very loyal and devoted to her husband in a special way, because he was her first love. The guy, on the other hand, was just getting started. He now had her in the sense of a conquest and, once conquered, was no longer interested. He treated her like a second-class person and then immediately cheated on her. After five years of infidelity, he divorced her for his secretary.

The wife was devastated and heart-broken and never remarried. She led a very frugal and simple life. She never got over the relationship and was never able to move on to someone else and seek happiness. Her friends and family encouraged her to go forward with her life, but she just knew in her heart he would come back to her.

The guy married his secretary and continued his unfaithfulness. Such a man is never satisfied. He divorced the secretary, found a third wife, and soon divorced her. After a couple of years he met his fourth wife. She was very sharp of wit and tongue. She was a real challenge because she was so difficult to deal with. After a lengthy and tumultuous courtship he finally wore her down—or so he thought. They got married without a pre-nuptial agreement. That was one of her conditions. Surprisingly, even after three divorces, he still had a sizable estate.

Once the marriage nuptials and honeymoon were over, the real marriage began. She started riding shotgun on his unfaithfulness and made his life a living hell.

The passage of time and life experiences will sometimes mature and soften the most recalcitrant of scoundrels. In this instance, four wives in 25 years changed the man forever. He started thinking of his first sweet wife and how happy they were when they got married. He realized he was a complete jerk. He knew in his heart this sweet woman, whose heart he had broken, was his only true love. He went back to her and confessed his love and mistakes.

Her prayers had been answered. She had endured so much well-intended advice during the years directing her to move on with her life. She was now rewarded for her faithfulness. He was back in her loving arms and she had never known greater joy. They confessed their love for each other and made plans to remarry. But first, he had to get rid of this last mistake of a wife.

This wife was a real fighter and was not going away easily. He hired the same lawyer who had represented him for the three previous divorces to start the fourth divorce procedure. The husband had been very successful financially. There was a business, a home, a condo at the beach, and a bundle of money at stake.

The fourth wife moved out of the house and took up residence at the beach condo. The husband was left alone in the homestead property. The first wife started visiting him on a regular basis. They were making plans for their remarriage and the rest of their life together.

Since the sweet wife had never really gotten on with her life, she had taken only small-paying jobs. She did not complete her education. She did not grow financially and, as a result, had virtually nothing. She was renting an apartment when her ex-husband came back into her life. He was her emotional and financial savior.

Divorces sometimes plod along slower than a fat snail on a Popsicle stick. This divorce was no exception. While making plans one night for their happy future, the husband started feeling a sharp pain in his side and started to vomit. The sweet wife took him to the hospital where he was thoroughly examined. After several agonizing days waiting for the results, the doctor finally called the husband into his office. The news was bleak. The inoperable pancreatic cancer had spread into the lymph node glands and the doctor said he had only months to live.

His physical condition deteriorated dramatically. He needed round the clock care and the sweet wife was the only one who cared for him. She quit her job and gave up her apartment and moved in the house with him to act as a 24-hour-a-day nursemaid. He said he loved her and would take care of her and after the divorce was final would make sure she was provided for financially. He called his attorney demanding action and was told the final divorce papers had been reviewed and approved by his fourth wife and her attorney. The Settlement Agreement and the Final Divorce Decree and had been sent to the judge for signing. All of his assets were jointly titled so the husband couldn't do anything with them until the judge signed the final order splitting the assets and giving him control over his share.

The ugly hand of fate slapped the sweet wife a second time. The final decree was sitting on the corner of the judges' desk waiting for a signature when the judge left that night. It would be signed in the morning with the rest of the papers in that pile. According to the doctors, the husband still had several months to live. No one thought this was a critical emergency. But as chance would have it, during the night, the husband died. The divorce decree was never signed by the judge. A divorce can't continue without two living spouses.

The soon to be fourth ex-wife was now the widow. Since all of the assets were jointly titled, they passed immediately to her. She owned and controlled everything. She jumped on the phone and called the first wife and said, "Get the hell out of my house." The fourth wife/widow was now also in control of the husband's body. The sweet wife knew the husband wanted his ashes spread over the gulf waters he loved so much and the fourth wife/widow knew this as well.

The fourth wife told everyone she honored his wishes by spreading his ashes over the gulf water in front of their condo. It is true that his ashes did make it to the gulf waters, however, it is rumored the widow said her good-byes to him while flushing him down the toilet.

Legal Analysis: *The husband could have drafted a new Will leaving control of his remains with his first wife. He could have executed a new Will, Health Care Surrogate and Durable Power of Attorney. He could have named this first wife as the beneficiary, but he didn't. Unfortunately, the assets in this case were all jointly owned and not separated until the final decree. Most divorce lawyers would want to separate the assets as soon as possible to avoid a situation such as this. Some states allow separation agreements before final divorce. Assets can be divided long before the final decree is signed. However, if the parties can't agree, the assets will remain in joint names until the judge signs the final order.*

I'm rich — and only 18 years old!

How can you spoil a child? I know one sure way. Give the child too much money, too soon.

"My problem is quite different from others you have probably dealt with," said the woman, one-half of a couple sitting at the table in my conference room.

"You'd be surprised what I've seen," I replied, remembering the client who asked me what would happen if he suddenly "disappeared in the Rapture." This lady before me looked quite pleasant and didn't appear to have any great problems. She said, "It's my daughter. She's 16, not very responsible and she will come into a lot of money very soon."

"How much?" I asked.

She flipped a recent brokerage statement across the table to me and commented, "There's over $900,000 in the account now and my broker projects it will grow to around $1.2 million by the time she turns 18."

I whistled. "That's a lot of money for an 18 year old."

The wife looked forlorned. "That's what I want to talk to you about. Is there any way we can hold on to that money and not let her have it all at age eighteen?"

"That depends," I said. "Tell me about the money."

Over the next twenty-five minutes my client explained that she had been married to another man and together, they had produced this daughter. They divorced when their daughter was two- years old. My client got custody but the child's father saw his daughter on a regular basis. Shortly thereafter, the father was killed in a car accident, but he had purchased a life insurance policy which contained a double indemnity clause. This clause allows the beneficiary to collect double the face value of the policy if the death is a result of an accident. He had named his two-year-old daughter as the sole beneficiary of the insurance policy and of his Will, which meant this toddler eventually received a check for $250,000.

In Florida, a minor's natural guardian, the parent, cannot control more than $15,000 of a minor's money. As a result, a guardianship was established naming a bank Trust department to control the investments. After fourteen years of very good returns, the guardianship account had grown to almost $900,000.

Mom said, "She's sixteen, and she knows about the money. She's a bright child and very independent, but lately she's been hanging around with the wrong children. You know the type—black outfits and tattoos and pierced body parts and all that. I don't want to sound like I'm freaked out or anything, but, well...I AM freaked out. Is there anything you can do to help?"

I reviewed the guardianship papers and told them their control of the assets was quite limited. "I'm surprised the judge even allowed you to invest the funds with a bank Trust department," I said. "Usually, Florida courts require the money stay in Treasury bills or certificates of deposit. The courts are very insistent that all of the money go to your daughter when she reaches the age of eighteen."

"But that's exactly what we don't want!" Mom said imploringly.

"I understand," I acknowledged, "but that's the law. In Florida, a minor can't hold assets greater than $15,000, which is why the guardianship account was set up. The court requires yearly reports to see how the accounts are doing. You remember all those child stars, and actors who grew up and discovered their parents had spent all of their money? Florida judges want to make sure that doesn't happen. They want to ensure the child gets all of the guardianship money when the child reaches the age of eighteen, no exceptions and no excuses. Some parents want to use the money to pay for things like food, cars and houses by rationalizing that the money is available, and the child will benefit from its use. But judges won't allow the ward's money to pay family expenses. If you don't have the money for a new car then you will just have to drive the old one as if the ward's money never existed. The courts require an annual accounting for the money and a formal closing of the guardianship when the ward reaches the age of eighteen. They usually want the guardianship accounts closed and paid out within a couple of months following the ward's eighteenth birthday. They want to see that signed release in the file indicating the ward got the money. What happens to the ward or what they do with the money after the check is received is irrelevant to them."

"But that's not right. She'll still be in High School. There must be something we can do," Mom pleaded.

"There is one possible option," I offered, "but I'm not sure it will work in your case. I can prepare an Irrevocable Trust that leaves you in control of your daughter's money until she reaches the age of thirty or thirty-five. You'll manage the money and use it for her benefit. Then when she reaches the age determined by the Trust, you terminate the Trust and give her the balance."

"That's what I want. That's it," gushed Mom. I held up my hand and she said, "There's a catch, isn't there?"

"There's always a catch," I said. "If it was this easy, who would need a lawyer?" She and her husband laughed. "The catch is that when your daughter reaches the age of eighteen, she must get the money. There's no away around it and you must prove to the court that she has complete control of the funds. Once this occurs, she has to voluntarily agree to place the money into an irrevocable Trust and relinquish her control. Only then will it be safe."

Mom had turned pale. "Oh my god!" she said. "You mean we have to tell her about this Trust and that she won't get the money until she reaches the age of thirty?"

I nodded. "Not only that, I have to thoroughly explain the terms of the Trust to her as well."

Mom slumped back in her chair. "She'll never go for that, she's already talking about what she is going to do with the money when she gets it. Isn't there some way we can trick her?"

"I'm sorry, she must know what she's signing, or the Trust will not be valid."

"This is going to ruin her life. There must be something I can do," She sat there in silence for several long minutes, and then sighed. "She'll never have a normal life now. It would have been better if her dad had left her nothing."

Legal Analysis: *Guardianship accounts must be released to the ward when the ward reaches the age of majority—eighteen—although some states may allow retention of the funds until the age of twenty-one. Unless the child is willing to have the funds kept in a continuing Trust account, the child will have full control of the money when they turn eighteen. In the above case, had her dad made the insurance money payable to his estate and created a Trust, the money could have been held by a family member or corporate Trustee. He could have kept the funds tied up in Trust until she reached 25 or 30 years of age. The Trustee could pay for the daughter's financial needs, including all school, college and post- graduate courses. The Trustee could also be given the authority to provide the daughter money to build a house, marry, or enter into a business or trade. The primary objective would be to keep the money out of the hands of a young and immature person.*

The generation following the Boomers, Generation X, is one of very liberal spenders. The thought of turning out a light, saving used foil, and washing a plastic cup is completely foreign to us. We just spend and charge until our credit is cut off, then we file bankruptcy and start over again.

Flinch test

I was a young lawyer fresh out of Law School, and meeting with my first two clients. I tried to appear as knowledgeable as possible to gain their confidence and answer their questions as best I could, but then they asked a question I couldn't answer. "How much does a Will cost?" I ducked the question and we discussed something else and after they left, I started drafting their documents. It was then I realized I was clueless as to how much to charge for Wills. They don't teach practical, nuts and bolts business topics in Law School. I could discuss at length and in depth the legal requirements for a Will, or the elements of negligence. But I couldn't tell anyone what a legal document costs.

I asked Ralph—the lawyer I was working for at the time—what to charge.

He said, "I'm going to tell you what an old lawyer told me when I asked the same question many years ago. You charge by using the flinch test."

"What in the world is that?"

Ralph took out two sheets of paper and said, "You present each client with their Wills." As Ralph said this he slid both sheets of paper across his desk as if they were the client's Wills. Then he said, "You look at them and say 'that will be one hundred dollars.' If they don't flinch, you say, 'for each.'"

I paid tax on money I didn't get

A mother and her daughter were in my office. Mom wanted to establish a Living Revocable Trust and make certain changes to her estate plan. She wanted the Trust set up so that her assets would be quickly and efficiently distributed to her two children without going through probate. The change she wanted to make to her estate plan included giving the home to her daughter along with one-half of her estate assets. The house was worth $300,000. The remaining assets consisted of cash in a bank account and a brokerage account that totaled about $600,000, so the entire estate had a value of approximately $900,000.

The mother was a pleasant lady. I told her, "I understand you want to give the house and one-half of your estate to your daughter. That means your daughter will get more than your son."

She smiled. "My daughter quit her job so that she could take care of me. She is with me every day. I want her to have the house and one-half of what is left in my estate."

"Okay," I said. "These are your assets and you can divide them in any manner you wish. However, I think it's in the best interest of your daughter that you talk to your son and explain how the estate is to be divided after your death. That way, your daughter will not be the bearer of bad news and your son won't think his sister was greedy and secretly influenced you for her own gain."

She shook her head. "Oh, no, I couldn't talk to him about this. He will be so upset."

I nodded in agreement, "Do you think it's fair to put your daughter in this awkward position? You need to call and talk to him. You know it's the right thing to do."

She reluctantly shook her head and said, "I'll call him." She didn't sound very convincing and I didn't believe she would do it.

Two years later the daughter called my office and reported her mother's death. She wanted to schedule a meeting, along with her brother, to review the terms of the Trust. At the meeting, it soon became apparent that the brother was in the dark about the changes his mother had made to the Trust. He had not seen the Trust nor had he been given any information about the estate. To my chagrin, I realized I was the one who would be the bearer of the bad news.

I started the meeting by saying, "According to the terms of the Trust, your sister gets the house. The residue or the rest of the estate is divided equally between you and your sister."

Clearly surprised, he said, "You mean my sister gets the house and half of the estate?! How much is the house worth?"

"About $300,000," I answered.

He stood up and then sat down, breathing hard. "That's not fair," he said angrily. "Why didn't Mom tell me about this?"

"I don't know. I told her to call you and explain what she was doing. Obviously, she didn't do it."

"No, she certainly did not."

Unfortunately, there was still more bad news.

"There is one more thing you should be aware of," I said. "The gift of the house to your sister goes to her with no consideration for estate taxes. That means that she gets the house, but what's left of the estate bears the burden of any inheritance taxes that may be due. And there are taxes due."

He stared at me. "What does that mean?"

"In a nutshell, it means you'll pay taxes on an asset you don't own or get."

He started to rant and rave and at one point I thought he was going to get up and leave. He finally settled down and seemed to take the rest of the meeting in stride, but he was definitely unhappy and much of his resentment was directed toward his sister. It would have been so much better if his mother had told him about the changes she made and her reason for those changes. But it was too late for that.

The brother still resents his sister. Once the estate was settled, he refused to have any further contact with her. Because of her mother's reluctance to deal with the problem when it could have been easily handled, the sister lost her brother and her children lost their uncle.

This situation is not unusual. Unfortunately, most clients are cowards. They leave unequal dispositions or leave a child out completely and don't tell the omitted child. That child is unpleasantly surprised, and where there's a surprise, there is usually a problem. I don't care how awful or neglectful a child has been to the parent, that child still expects an inheritance. Memories are very selective. Don't assume the child should know they are omitted from the Will. Some clients discuss this issue with their children, but usually only the dad will do this. I have yet to meet a mom who will call a child and say, "by the way, I'm leaving you out my Will." (Even the woman in "My Son Married an Older Woman" wouldn't call her son and let him know he was being omitted from the Will). If they can't deal with the omitted child face to face, I encourage clients to at least leave a letter explaining their position. Put in writing why a child has been omitted or had their share of the estate reduced. Don't leave this burden for your other children.

Legal Analysis: *Estate Attorneys want their documents to withstand legal challenges, but would prefer never to have a document challenged, such as in a Will contest or Trust contest. In my opinion, if all family members are aware of who's in and who's out, the likelihood of a legal challenge is reduced. The time to deal with problem children is when the client is living, so that answers and explanations can be provided. Avoiding the confrontation and putting off the bad news only makes it worse for the ones you leave behind.*

Party on me

"I don't have any kids so I want to be remembered by my friends. I don't want them crying over me. I want them to have a party, a big party. How much money do you think a big party will cost?" asked my client.

"Well, it depends on whether or not I'm invited," I replied.

She laughed. "I don't think everyone needs Dom Perignon champagne, but they could drink some nice beer in my honor."

"I think a couple thousand dollars would be sufficient for a nice party."

She nodded, "Then that's what I want to do. Put in the Will that the Personal Representative will use $5000 to put on a party for my friends. I'm giving all of my money to charity anyway. Who cares if they get a few dollars less? I want to be remembered for something special by my friends. I want them to think of me in a way that makes them laugh."

> ***Legal Analysis:*** *You can direct the Personal Representative to do just about anything. This is the third such Will I drafted where a PR had been given instructions to use estate assets for a going-away party.*

My son's widow has all of my money

After one of my workshops, an attendee talked to me about his father.

"Dad is 93 and he's got a little bit of a problem."

"Is he mentally and physically okay?"

"Oh yeah, he's fit as a fiddle. I think he's in better shape than me. But that's not the problem. The problem involves money and Medicaid planning."

"Why don't you start from the beginning. That way I can get all the facts and hopefully provide you with a better answer."

He related his story. "Dad has been very healthy all of his life. He has attended several workshops about estate planning. Recently, he went to one concerning the Medicaid spend-down. He was pretty upset when he left the workshop after learning all of his assets must be used to pay for his nursing home expense, except the last two thousand dollars. He would be destitute and leave nothing to pass down to his children. I don't care if I get any money from my father's estate. Most of my brothers and sisters don't care either. However, I know it's really important to him to leave an inheritance. The problem started when he decided to do some of his own planning after reading a book about Medicaid. He wanted to avoid the Medicaid spend-down. So he transferred all of his assets to my brother, who lives in the same town, just a few blocks away from Dad. Anyway, Dad gave my brother all of his cash and securities. The amount was around $500,000. This was back when Dad was 89, about four years ago. They had an understanding. Dad used his income to pay for his expenses and if he needed anything else, my brother would use Dad's money to get it, pretty smooth sailing."

I interjected, "I think I know what is coming."

He agreed. "You're right, it's the worst thing that could have happened. My brother died."

"Did your brother have the money tied up in a Trust or some other protective legal instrument?"

"No, I don't think so. Dad just transferred the money to my brother. I never heard of any special Trusts or anything like that. My brother had the investments titled in his name so the three-year Medicaid time limit could pass. The time period did pass and Dad is eligible for Medicaid. I know they talked about it. I just don't think they planned on my brother dying first. But now that he's gone, Dad has a big problem."

"Let me guess. Your brother's wife got all of your dad's money and now she doesn't want to give it up."

"That's right," he said. "You must have seen this before. My dad wants to know how he can get his money back."

I gritted my teeth. "Your father now wants his money back?"

He looked at me hopefully. "That's right. How can he get it back?"

Shaking my head, I answered, "I'm not sure he can get it back. He gave it to your brother with no strings attached. It was a gift. Your brother died and didn't leave the money in a Will or Trust held for Dad's use. I hope she's having a good time with the money."

He rolled his eyes. "That's part of the problem. She's already seeing another guy. It's her personal fitness instructor. Dad said if he was just a few years younger he'd open a can of Whoop-ass and take care of the situation. But I guess he'll never get any of his money back?"

I agreed, "No. Not unless she feels sorry for him and just gives it to him out of the kindness of her heart. And that doesn't seem likely, does it?"

"Not really. Especially since Dad already demanded it back and she just laughed. I think she saw her lawyer within hours after my brother's death."

Legal Analysis: *A gift is a gift. Once given, it's gone. This tragic result could have been avoided with proper planning. After receiving the money, the son could have created a Living Revocable Trust and placed this money in it. The Trust would have protected the money in case of divorce. Further, in case of death, Dad would have been the only beneficiary and special language in the Trust would keep the money from the grasp of Medicaid and the widow.*

Dad's a pig

"My dad's dead and I hate him. I still can't believe what he did," hissed my client. I sat there wondering what could bring a fifty-six year-old man to this point and asked him what had happened to make him feel this way.

"I gave up my life to work for my father in our family business," he snapped. "I could have done a lot with my life, but I gave it all up. So how am I repaid for my years of work and sacrifice? My dad slaps me in the face by giving our family company, the one I helped build, to my son."

"Maybe he did that for estate tax reasons," I responded.

He shook his head. "No, I don't think so. He never really respected me. I put all that time into the business, but he never really respected me."

"If your son owns the business, what's the problem?"

"My son and I don't get along," he said. "My dad always undermined my authority with him and now it's a real problem."

"I'm sure it can't be that bad."

"Oh, yeah," he yelled, "He fired me! My own son fired me from my company. Now I don't have a job and I don't have the security I thought I would have. This should be the time in my life when I can relax a bit and enjoy life, but I've got to look for a job."

I was stunned and said, "This is unfortunate. Did he do this on purpose?"

"I don't know if he did or not," he said, "but one thing is for sure—I'll never forgive him. He's a pig."

Legal Analysis: *Point 1: There is no legal requirement that you leave a child any inheritance. However, in order to omit a child, one must have a Will or a Trust. The document must acknowledge the child and expressly omit him or her. Most states do not require that the Testator leave the child one dollar or some other* *monetary amount. However, an estate planning attorney should be consulted before this is attempted.*

Point 2: Some clients simply wish to leave an inheritance to a grandchild. This story highlights several reasons why this planning can cause problems. If a large gift is made, the parent of the child loses all parental control. How can you control your son if he has more money than you and owns the company you work for? The jealousy factor can also ruin a relationship between a parent and their child.

You don't know me, but you're my Dad!

When you were young and wild, sowing seeds in every pretty field that crossed your path, did you keep track of every girl? Ever wonder what happened to them? Did you ever consider the possible consequences of all that sowing? A client of mine learned first-hand what the consequences could be.

Sitting across the table from me in my office conference room one afternoon, he told me his story.

"It was early in the evening when the doorbell rings. I'm watching 'Wheel of Fortune,' and I know the answer: Komodo Dragon. I'm thinking about a Komodo Dragon and I push myself out of my Lazy Boy recliner and walk to the front door. I open it and there is an older woman standing there. I'm 74 and she looks to be late 50's or so. She says, 'Are you [John Smith]?' I said I was and she said, 'You don't know me, but you're my father.'"

"Father, Komodo Dragon, Wheel of Fortune—my mind felt as though it was awash in a thick fuzzy soup and all I could do was stare at her. She said, 'I'm sorry, let me back up a bit. Did you live at 54 Elm Street in Allentown, Pennsylvania?' I nodded. 'Do you remember a girl named Sue, who lived three doors down from you?'"

"Like a thunderbolt, the memory came flooding back. My heart was pounding, and the blood in my veins felt like a fireman's hose on full pressure. One more notch up and it was going to burst. I felt dizzy as I remembered what had happened so many years ago. I was 14 and Sue was 16. Finally I said, 'Why don't you come in?' She did and I introduced her to my wife."

I shook my head. "Unbelievable," I said. "There was no warning? No letter? No call? Just out of the blue she shows up on your doorstep and says, 'I'm your daughter?'"

"That's right, and I nearly had a coronary on the spot."

"You were 14 when you met this 16 year-old-girl. And you had sex with her?"

"We only did it once, and then she went away and I didn't see her again." He sighed. "I have a family now. How is this going to affect my wife and children? Is she going to get any of my estate?"

"It's not really a problem," I said. "Now that you are aware of her, I will amend your Trust document. You acknowledge her as your daughter—in writing—and simply say she receives nothing from your estate. There is no requirement here in Florida that you leave her one dollar or some other token amount, but you must at least acknowledge her and say she gets nothing."

"Do you think she is after my assets?"

"I doubt it. In my experience, most children searching for a missing parent just want to see where they came from, what their Dad looks like, how he thinks, how he has lived his life. They want to share their life with their parent. Money is not the motivation."

He said, "What if I don't want this relationship?"

"You can't be forced to have a relationship with anyone," I offered. "It's up to you, but what does your wife think about this?"

He shook his head, "She wasn't too thrilled at first, but I think she is resigned to the fact that I made a mistake as a young boy. I think she's okay with it now, but it was touch and go for a while until all of the facts came out. Luckily, this new daughter has been very nice and not too pushy, but my wife still thinks she's after our estate."

After discussing this situation with my client, I went home and that evening mentioned it to my wife. We have been married 23 years and I asked her what she would do if a woman suddenly appeared at our front door claiming to be my daughter.

My wife looked at me and said, "As long as she is older than 23, it won't be a problem!"

Legal Analysis: *If you know about an illegitimate child, and want them omitted from your estate, you can mention him or her by name in your Will. You are not required to leave any estate assets to a child you raised and certainly not to one you just met.*

In another case, a client admitted he had been a real lady's man and didn't know how many children he might have sired. I drafted the Will and inserted a sentence that indicated he had carefully considered all of his known children and wanted any and all unknown children omitted. I told him I was not sure it would work in every state but, it did give his new wife some piece of mind.

Mom's last wish

For the past ten years, I have done a Saturday morning radio show. It's a call-in lawyer's show on estate planning during which I answer questions on estate planning issues.

Recently, a pleasant-sounding young man called.

He began, "I hope you can help me. I don't know what else to do." He said his family had always been close and about a year ago his mother, brother, and sister had a family meeting. His mother told them she had a terminal illness and had about six months to live.

He continued, "As you can imagine, the news was a great shock because we didn't expect it. Mom had few assets, and she did not want anything to go through probate. The bank account had next to nothing in it and her only asset of value was the house. Her last wish was for the three of us to be added to her deed, so we would all own it and share in the sale proceeds after her death. My sister and I did not want our names on the deed for our own reasons. My brother agreed to have his name added so we had a quit-claim deed prepared adding my brother as co-owner with rights of survivorship. That way, when mom died, he would own it without having to go through probate. We agreed that after Mom died, my brother would sell the house and the proceeds would be divided among the three of us."

I said, "Well, what happened?"

The caller responded, "Mom died several months ago, but my brother refused to sell the house and divide the proceeds as previously agreed."

I asked, "Did you ask him why he's not selling the house and dividing the proceeds?"

The caller said, "I asked him that very question. My brother said, 'When you and Lisa left, Mom told me she wanted me to have the house.'"

"How can my brother do that?" the caller demanded. "The Will says that all of the assets are to be divided in three shares."

I explained the Will only controls assets that pass through probate. "The house is now owned by your brother and is not controlled by the Will. It's his house and he can do with it as he pleases," I said.

There was silence on the phone and for a moment, I thought he had hung up. Finally he blurted, "That's not fair."

"You're right," I said. "Sometimes life isn't fair. You can always hire a lawyer and sue him and try to set aside the transfer, but your chances of success are not good."

"Well he can just keep the house and rot in Hell for all I care." He took a deep breath. "Thanks for your help," he said, and hung up.

To the listening audience I said, "This call is a perfect example of how adding a name to a deed with rights of survivorship can lead to family problems. Yes, the survivorship deed avoided probate, but the result is a situation where the children will probably never talk to each other again. Is that worth it? Is avoiding probate worth the termination of your children's relationship?"

Legal Analysis: *A Will only controls the assets that pass through probate. All joint accounts titled with rights of survivorship pass to the surviving joint owner. Many people have added a child to an account or deed so the child can write checks, access accounts and avoid probate. If a parent has only one child and the child doesn't have any judgments or liens against them, it might be okay to add their name to an account or deed. However, my experience has led me to discourage clients from this type of estate planning, except in rare situations.*

A good catch

Some women are lonely after the death of a spouse or after a divorce. Some will be in the market for a new husband. If so, a retried Air Force officer is a good catch. Most career officers are decent men. They made it through the 20 plus year career in the military to reach the point where they can retire. They have moved often and put up with a lot of inconveniences. Most are real men. They like to fish, hunt, play golf and engage in other "manly" sports. And most want the company of a nice, lovely, doting wife. They want to take care of a woman like this and will provide for her needs. Most of these military men are still fit and like to go places and do things. They're not couch potatoes. They've been all over the world in their careers and they still like to travel.

They may not have created a giant financial nest egg, but they do have a permanent military retirement income. The check arrives in their account on the first of every month. A retired career officer will receive between $3000 and $7000 monthly—spendable cash. They do not need to save because this amount is adjusted upward for inflation plus they receive regular military pay raises. If they live within their monthly income they can go anywhere and do anything they want with little concern for their future needs. Their healthcare needs are covered by the military's medical insurance program (Tri-Care). They also receive additional benefits if they live near a military base, such as shopping at the base commissary and Base Exchange.

One of my military clients and his wife saw me 5 years ago. I completed a Trust package including a Living Revocable Trust, Will, Healthcare Surrogate, Living Will, and Power of Attorney. Two years later the wife died of cancer. Following his wife's death, my client met me for a review of his estate plan. We made the necessary changes and separated the Trust into the A (Above ground) and the B (Below ground- credit shelter) Trust. During this time he was having difficulties coping with the loss of his wife. He was constantly depressed, lonely, and in tears. He had never experienced anything quite like this and was not sure how he could go on with his life. I spent several hours with him telling him these feelings were normal. After the loss of a spouse there are several stages of emotional recovery. This grieving process follows a standard pattern. If this is explained in the proper way, most can understand and not give up hope. For those who lose a spouse or child, and don't believe in God, I truly feel sorry. Where does your wife go once gone from this world? This type of loss is very difficult because of the uncertainty. Those who believe in God and the afterlife can gain some comfort knowing the one they lost is no longer suffering but is in heaven and happy.

Sometimes the work I do is not necessarily legal. Oftentimes it is counseling those with a loss. In this case, the client was distraught. "Mark, I know what you are saying. I know intellectually I will be okay, but, emotionally, I'm not sure I can make it."

I said, "If you just hold on and live one day at a time you will make it. You never know, the next time you see me it may be to do a pre-nuptial agreement for a new wife."

That brought a hint of a smile to his face. "I don't know when I will ever be able to date again. This is really tough. I don't wish this situation on anyone." He left my office. The work he requested was completed and I didn't see him for another year.

After not seeing him or hearing from him for more than a year, he called my office in high spirits. "Mark, you were right. I've met someone and we're going to get married."

"That's great," I responded, "who's the lucky gal?"

"My son introduced me to her several months ago. I don't think anyone thought we would get along so well. We really seemed to click. She has been single for five years. After several dinners and a lot of time together, we both came to the same conclusion—why wait?'"

"So when are you getting married?" I asked.

"As soon as you can get the pre-nuptial agreement drawn up," he laughed.

"You remembered my advice," I said.

"This romance has made my head spin, but it hasn't left me stupid. I still want to protect my children. I intend to take care of her, but my main focus will be my children. Anyway, she has her own money, almost as much as me, and she wants to leave it to her son," he explained.

I said, "I'll get right on it and have a draft of the pre-nuptial agreement in a week or two. By the way, have you checked into your SBP (survivors benefit annuity plan) benefits for your new wife?"

He said, "No, I haven't really thought about it."

"You should call the Base benefits department. If you qualify, your new wife can get 35% to 50% of your retirement pay for the rest of her life. It would be a shame to let that benefit go unused, considering you paid in for 20 years and then never used it because your first wife predeceased you," I offered.

"That would be great," he said, "I will get on it right away. That sure would be a great benefit if it's still available."

We met a week later and he reported his findings. "Mark, you were right. The benefits department informed me that I can re-enroll in the SBP program and protect my new wife. I was afraid they would make me pay in a lump sum for the time missed since my first wife died. But they said I just needed to enroll after I am married and they will deduct the same amount from my retirement check. Then after my death, my new wife will receive the SBP amount, about $2600, for the rest of her life."

I said, "That's great. What a wonderful benefit for her. She will receive a permanent income stream for the rest of her life. It would have been a shame to waste that benefit after you paid in for so many years."

"That is quite a bit of money," he pondered.

I smiled, "You didn't know you were such a great catch, did you?"

He slowly replied with a wry smile, "No, I didn't really think about it. But now that you mention it, I'm not that cute and she is awful good looking.' Makes you wonder, doesn't it?"

Legal Analysis: *The survivor benefit program is a great benefit for a military spouse. It can be reactivated most of the time for a new spouse. Even a divorced retired military man might be entitled to some or all of the SBP benefits. The children can get all of the assets but the new wife can get a permanent income for the rest of her life. It's a win–win situation.*

If I sign that Will, I'll die

A lady lost her husband as the result of a car accident. He died without a Will and left a big mess for her and his children. He intended his current wife to receive all of his estate assets. Unfortunately, in Florida, when you die without a Will the laws of intestacy govern what happens. Each state has such laws to govern the distribution of a person's estate if they die without a Will. The American Bar Association estimates that as many as 70% of United States citizens do not have a Will.

The laws in Florida hold that if you die without a Will the estate assets (those assets titled solely in the name of the decedent) will be distributed in a certain way. If the decedent was married with children only produced from that marriage, then the surviving spouse gets the use of the homestead (the house where they live), $60,000, and 50% of the rest. The remaining 50% goes to the children immediately. If the decedent has children from a prior marriage, which in this case he did, the surviving wife gets a life estate in the homestead (a right to live in the house for the rest of her life) and splits the estate 50/50. She does not get the first $60,000.

This lady was very disgusted with her husband for dying and leaving her with such a mess. His children from three prior marriages are now heirs in their father's estate. Most of the children have not seen or talked to their dad in many years. When he met his fourth wife, he was destitute. All assets he accumulated occurred while married to this fourth wife. For some reason, there were several assets not titled in their joint names.

Another odd problem cropped up, resulting from the manner of his death. He was killed in an automobile accident. His estate has the right to claim net accumulations. This is simply the loss of the continued savings he might have accumulated had he lived. Since he had no Will, this amount will be shared between his wife and his six other children. Had he lived, there is no doubt he would have wanted his wife to have this. All their accounts were joint and she would have received all of this had he lived. However, he didn't live and he left no Will. A simple Will would have eliminated all of these problems. He would have said, "All I have, I give to my wife, if she survives me; if she doesn't survive me, then to my children in equal shares.' Since his wife survived him, all estate assets would have gone to her with no involvement by the other estranged kids.

The point I'm trying to make concerns the surviving wife. She saw the problems created because her husband died with no Will. I talked to her several times about executing a Will so she would not repeat the problem for her kids.

She said, "I know I need to do this. Let me think about it for a while and I will call you to set up a date."

I said, "What's to think about? You told me you wanted to split your estate among your children and the grandson living with you." She is raising a grandson because her son is in jail.

"I know," she deferred. "I just want to think about it and get back with you."

"All right, but don't leave your kids with the same mess your husband left you," I warned.

Several months later she still had not signed her Will. She was in the hospital for routine examinations. The doctors found several massive inoperable tumors. When I learned about this I called and offered to visit the hospital to get the Will signed. She still refused. She confided to my secretary that she thought signing the Will would somehow hasten her death. She wanted to wait until she got out of the hospital to sign the Will. I think she thought if she put off that task she couldn't die until it was finished. Unfortunately for her children and particularly, her grandson, that was foolish thinking. She slipped into a coma several days later and died without ever signing a Will. She never made her last wishes legally known. The grandson she wanted to include is not included; the son in jail gets a share. What a mess. This mess could have been easily avoided. It's not like she wasn't aware of the consequences. She had just suffered them at her husband's death several months earlier. They were still fresh on her mind. Maybe she just wanted her family to fight over her, as her last selfish deed.

Legal Analysis: *Statistically, the signing of a Will does not hasten death. On the contrary, most of my clients leave my office feeling a great burden has been lifted. They are happy and very relieved. Most look at me and say "This is it? It's done?" I respond, "Yes, it's pretty painless, isn't it?" Those who know the* *consequences and still do no planning are just selfish. This is not my sentiment, it's the sentiment of those left to deal with the mess, such as in the situation above. Some simply don't realize the consequences. There are many books, workshops, and tapes that can provide easy-to-grasp concepts about simple and proper estate planning.*

According to the American Bar Association, 70% of U.S. citizens <u>do not</u> have a Will.

Casserole queens

After we discussed the relevant estate matters, I talked to my client about how to move forward with her life. She had lost her husband five years before and I asked if she had ever thought about dating again.

She gave me a conspiratorial smile and said, "I've got to ask you a question. When is it appropriate to talk to a man who has lost his wife? I mean, how long should you wait before you… you know, go over for a visit and bring him a casserole?"

"Good gosh," I said, "I have no idea, I've never really thought about it. How about four or five months?" I offered.

She said, "Let me tell you what happened to me. I've known this man and his wife at our church for the past five or six years. My husband knew of him, but he and his wife have always been just acquaintances, nothing more. After my husband died, I continued going to church. I saw this man and his wife on a regular basis, but we just passed in the hallway. We never had lunch or anything like that. I always thought he was just the nicest man. Then his wife developed cancer and died last year. I thought to myself, I would like to get to know him a little better, but I don't want to go over too soon. You know, that would be… tacky."

"I can imagine," I said.

She continued, "A friend told me he liked chicken pot pie casseroles. I thought I would wait about six weeks and then take over a nice chicken pot pie casserole to his house." She stopped and looked at me. Her eyes were smiling.

With anticipation, I said, "Well, what happened?"

She said, "I had the casserole in my right hand sitting on an oven mitt. It was hot and fresh from my oven and it smelled heavenly. I knocked on the door and he answered after about 30 seconds. As he opened the door, I could see into his kitchen and noticed the kitchen table. There was a casserole already sitting on the table. And as I walked in I noticed another woman firmly entrenched in his family room."

She laughed, snapped her fingers and said, "I waited too long. Another woman beat me to him."

We're not married, but don't tell the kids

The meeting with the older couple was going smoothly with no major problems so far. This couple was in a second marriage. She had two children by her first marriage, as did he. The estate planning issues seemed fairly straight-forward and uncomplicated.

Then the wife dropped the bombshell. Looking a little embarrassed she said. "There is one other thing."

"What's that?"

"We're not married."

It took a minute for my brain to register this information. "But you both have the same last name."

"Yes I know," said the wife, "I had my last name legally changed to his. You're only the fourth person to know this. Our kids don't even know!"

"This new information presents several interesting estate issues," I said. "The main one being that when one of you dies, there will be no marital deduction. That means if [Frank] dies first, inheritance taxes will be due immediately. Another potential issue is the control of the body after death. The survivor would have no rights."

They looked at each other. "We didn't think about that," she said. "Well, that's why we're here. We want you to help us fix those problems."

I glanced at their records. "Is there a compelling reason why you're not married?"

She continued, "When my first husband died, I received his military retirement. If I remarry, I lose $24,000 per year. Frank and I have discussed it and we don't think the benefits of marriage outweigh the extra $24,000 per year. We use that money to take trips and do other things we couldn't afford. But we don't think the kids would approve of us 'living in sin,' so I legally changed my last name and told them we got married."

I nodded. "I can prepare a Trust for each of you so the survivor is in control after the first spouse dies. This will minimize the potential inheritance tax problem. Documents such as the Durable Power of Attorney and the Health Care Surrogate allow each of you to control the other's financial and medical decisions. The Will can direct what should be done with the bodily remains so the survivor can control that situation as well. The Trust will allow the survivor to control the decedent's assets and benefit from the income and financial resources but also provide some assurances that the decedent's children will receive an inheritance."

She sighed, "That's exactly what we need."

"I will also need to modify all the documents to remove the words spouse, husband, and wife, and use your names instead. It will not be obvious in the documents that you are not married. On other occasions I have used the phrase, 'my friend' instead of spouse, but I don't think that would be appropriate in your case."

That's what we want," she said. "We want control over each other, but most of all, we want our privacy."

Legal Analysis: *The control of a deceased body usually rests with the family. The wife has first rights to control it unless there is a specific designation in the Will. However, some Wills are not probated until long after a person is buried, and are consequently of little use.*

This situation is most prominent when gay and lesbian couples or life partners lose a "spouse." The decedent's disapproving family often rushes in and controls the funeral and burial and may even exclude the partner. Further, if the estate is not properly set-up, the surviving partner may face immediate eviction from the joint residence. The use of joint titles, a Will, and Trust can prevent these problems. A Durable Power of Attorney and a Designation of Health Care Surrogate can give the healthy partner the legal rights to control all legal and health care decisions for a sick partner.

For the unmarried couple in my story, their Trusts would protect the surviving "spouse" and the decedent's children. The Trust established by the decedent allowed the surviving partner to use the money at the survivor's death, but directed that the Trust money, ultimately, go to the decedent's children.

An individual who turns age 65 has a 43 percent chance of spending some time in a nursing home.

I hate lawyers and the IRS

The old codger was terminally ill and he knew it, but he wasn't going to go easily. His loathing of the IRS and of lawyers seemed to energize him.

"I hate the bastards," he said to his friend. "If I never see another lawyer and never pay another dime in taxes, I'll die a happy man."

"Well," his friend replied, "You know what they say, 'you can't avoid death and taxes.' The lawyers are there at death for probate and the IRS gets their last bite at the apple when you die with estate taxes."

The old codger looked slyly at his friend and said. "I fixed it so there won't be no stinking lawyers after I'm gone. Best of all, the IRS gets screwed."

"How did you manage that?"

"I got it all fixed up," he said. "I've got about 3 million in assets and they're all in CDs, annuities, and savings bonds. I also have bank accounts and several brokerage accounts. Since I don't have any children, I'm giving my estate to my nieces and nephews and of course, Maggie, my lady friend. I've placed a 'POD'—that means Payable on Death—designation on the bank and brokerage account. Maggie and I have several joint accounts where the survivor gets the account. Also, the house is jointly owned so she'll get that too when I die." He smiled. "I've taken care of everything. All of my assets go where I want them to go without the damn lawyers getting a penny. Since no one is getting more than a couple hundred thousand dollars the IRS doesn't get anything either."

The friend looked concerned. "Are you sure that's the way it works? I thought it was the total amount of the estate that counted, not what each individual got."

"Hey, I don't give a shit about their stupid rules," he chuckled. "Those bastards aren't getting another dime from me."

A year later the old guy died and his friend was pleasantly surprised to learn his name was on a $200,000 CD. He contacted his accountant and asked if there was anything he needed to do about receiving the money. The reply was "I'm not sure. You'd better see a lawyer."

The friend sought the advice of an estate tax lawyer who was not pleased with what he found.

"What a mess," the lawyer said, shaking his head. "You were right to think there might be a problem. The IRS looks at the total amount of the decedent's estate, not what he gave to each heir. Your share was $200,000 and that amount alone does not trigger a tax, but if the estate was larger than the unified credit, $1,000,000 (in 2004 the credit amount increased to $1,500,000) a 706 Estate and Gift Tax Return is due along with the tax payment. Since you received an inheritance and know or have reason to believe the estate amount is greater than $1 million dollars, you should initiate a 706 filing. That way you will only be liable for your proportional share of the taxes and not penalties. Further, you may also shield yourself from possible criminal penalties for tax evasion. I doubt that is likely but you never know. Do you know the names of all of the other beneficiaries receiving assets?"

"No, I only know the names of a few, including Maggie, his lady friend. Maybe she'll know the names of the rest of the heirs."

After several weeks of digging, the estate lawyer met again with his client to discuss the progress on the estate matter.

"I think we have located most of the heirs," related the lawyer. "I tell you, they are a tight-lipped bunch of characters. I wasn't able to get much information from them except to confirm the receipt of assets from the decedent. However, not one person would tell me how much they got. I told them I needed to know the amount they received in order to determine the taxable estate. The taxable estate size would allow me to determine their share due the IRS, since it was likely each would have to contribute a proportional share of their inheritance for taxes."

"How did they react?"

The lawyer laughed, "Not very enthusiastically. Most seemed to think the taxes and the accounting were someone else's problem. Several mentioned they had consulted their own lawyers."

"So what's the next step?"

"For your own protection, you should file an incomplete 706 Estate Tax Return notifying the IRS about the estate and the amount you received along with the names of any other known beneficiaries. This relieves you of any potential criminal sanctions for tax evasion. The IRS will use its resources to ferret out the other beneficiaries and come to some agreement as to the total amount of the estate. Hopefully, you'll have to pay only your proportional share of the taxes, but that could be as much as 45% of your inheritance. That would be about $90,000 from your $200,000 CD. You told me your friend had an estate estimated at 3 million dollars. The current unified credit allows a deduction of $1,000,000 dollars ($1,500,000 in 2004 and 2005). You subtract the $1,000,000 from the total estate of $3 million and this leaves a taxable estate of $2,000,000. That means each beneficiary must pay the IRS a 45% proportional share of his or her inheritance. Unfortunately, it appears that several heirs have been spending this money with no regard for the taxes and some of them may end up owing back taxes, penalties and interest."

Stunned by this cascade of bad news, the friend was in shock. Finally he said, "This is truly unbelievable. I never imagined there would be so many issues and potential problems. [Ralph] seemed so sure there would be no problems. Obviously, he was dead wrong."

Several months later the friend met with his lawyer, who told him, "It turns out there were eight beneficiaries, including his lady friend, Maggie. Each now has his or her own lawyer. The IRS is sniffing around and they're bound to dig up something. They may charge the estate with extra penalties, but I'm not sure at this point. The bottom line here is that this has been a very profitable case for the eight lawyers involved and it could drag on for years."

His friend shook his head. "Who would have thought it could get this bad?"

"I'm not finished."

"There's more?"

The lawyer nodded. "One of the beneficiaries spent all of his inheritance, including the tax dollars. He says he didn't know about the tax. It's all gone now. Needless to say, the IRS can't get blood out of a turnip so it will require the remaining beneficiaries, including you, to pay his share."

The friend was astonished. "You're kidding me. Can they make me pay for his taxes?"

"Absolutely. They can and they will. This has turned out to be one of the biggest estate blunders I've seen in years. It's not the fault of the estate lawyers or the IRS. If your friend had done even minimal estate planning, he could have avoided all this. One lawyer could have easily taken care of his estate. Now he's paying for eight lawyers. Instead of reducing the tax burden he has significantly increased it. This is a textbook case on how to create an estate where lawyers and the IRS are the biggest beneficiaries. I wonder who got the last laugh?"

Differences between men and women

I have noticed a trend concerning sons and daughters. Frequently, a client will bring a child along to the estate planning meeting. After I review the client's estate assets, I ask where they want all of these assets to go after they are gone. Most clients say to their children, in equal shares. The children sitting there usually nod and agree. That was the agreed plan. Then I say "If your child predeceases you, where do you next want the assets to go?" Whoops, they haven't thought of that yet. This is where the difference between sons and daughters appears.

If the child is a son, he will think about his wife and children. If a daughter, she will think only about her children. A son in a long-term marriage wants his share to go to his wife, so that she can use it, control it, and give it to their children at her death. The daughter does the opposite. She doesn't want her husband to have the money. After her death, he could get remarried and give it to some young bimbo. The daughters usually feel the husband would be fine as the Trustee of the money, but rarely as the beneficiary.

Charge her with harassment

"If my daughter calls again, I want you to charge her with harassment," my client said. "She is causing a terrible problem for me at home."

"What's she doing?"

My client's face turned red and the angry words came in a rush. "She's ruining my marriage and has no right to do that. I made a mistake 48 years ago, and I don't want it to ruin my marriage now." He took a deep breath, obviously trying to control his temper. "I don't have to see her, do I?"

"I'll do what I can, but it's hard to keep a child from writing you or calling. Is she threatening you in any way?"

"No, she's not threatening me. It's my marriage I'm worried about."

"How is she ruining your marriage?"

"My wife thinks she wants to take our estate. She thinks this daughter is after my assets."

"In my experience, grown children like your daughter want only one thing. They want to get to know their parent and share their lives with them. I have yet to see a lost child who was motivated solely by greed."

"Well, I have a life too," he said, "and she is causing a lot of stress to me and my wife. If I wanted to maintain a relationship with her I would have done so. I never have wanted a relationship, and I don't want one now."

Legal Analysis: *This was another case where I amended the Trust document naming the "lost" child and directed that she or her issue receive nothing from the estate. There is no requirement that you leave even one dollar to a child if you choose not to. However, you must acknowledge the child. Many jurisdictions permit you to say something like, "I acknowledge I have a son, John, but I direct that he and his issue receive nothing from my estate."*

This case further emphasizes the point that many parents do not want to be found. Although a child may have a strong yearning to find a parent to fill a missing void, the child should be prepared for rejection. The parent may have a nice comfortable family and not want or appreciate the emotional upheaval to him and his family caused by the sudden appearance of a long-lost child.

In the next 10 years, 10 to 12 trillion dollars will change hands from the oldest generation to the next generation down. That is more money changing hands than has changed hands during the entire 200 year history of our country.

Can I sue myself if I'm my own lawyer?

A rich, elderly gentleman married my client's mother. She had little money and my client said she married him because of the security the old codger would provide. He lived in a lovely waterfront home, drove the latest model Cadillac and dined out frequently. It was a great lifestyle. He wanted female companionship, but still wanted all his money to go to his kids. He was not really concerned with his wife's well-being after his death or providing financial security for her. "She didn't have anything when I met her and she's not getting any of my kid's money when I'm gone," he told friends. He gave her a small allowance, but required that she keep a record of every penny she spent. She couldn't even buy a toaster without his express approval. He refused to allow her to keep any money or have her own little stash of "mad" money for even small personal items. He controlled and dominated her with his checkbook.

The old guy was not only stingy with his wife but didn't want to spend any money on lawyers for estate advice or a pre-marital agreement either. He decided the only asset his wife would receive at his death was the waterfront home. He titled the home in both their names and constantly told her how fortunate she was that he was allowing her to get the home after his death, often reminding her that "I don't have to leave you a damn thing." But he wasn't really being that generous— she didn't have the income or other resources to pay for the taxes, insurance, and maintenance. She would be forced to sell the house immediately.

He was a self-made man and rarely asked anyone for help. He did his own reading about Living Revocable Trusts in a book he got from the library. The book explained how to avoid probate and control assets after death. The book said that if the estate assets are controlled by the Trust after death, they will be distributed directly to the children without going through probate. This transfer of assets would occur without the wife being able to claim a spouse's elective share. In Florida, an omitted spouse can claim up to thirty percent of the estate assets passing through probate. However, if the assets are held in a Living Revocable Trust, the assets avoid probate and the spouse could not claim the thirty percent share. (This rule changed in 2001 and now the surviving spouse can claim the elective share amount of 30% from trust assets as well as probate assets.)

From his reading, the old guy learned enough about the law to make himself dangerous. He put together his own Trust and had his secretary type up the Trust documents. He was quite pleased for being so clever and saving a couple thousand dollars in attorney fees.

After several years, the old guy croaked and his family swooped in to take control of the estate assets. That's when they learned the old man had failed to title the estate assets in the name of the Trust, a basic principal every Trust lawyer understands. Unfortunately for the family, their Dad refused to hire a lawyer. Fortunately for the wife, the assets passed through probate before making it to the Trust which meant she could claim her thirty percent share. When everything was settled, she ended up with about $900,000 and the house, in which she now can afford to live.

She later told me, "He was so stingy I think if he had discovered his mistake, he would have sued himself."

Legal Analysis: *Most states have rules governing a surviving spouse's right to a share of the estate and most of these rules allow the spouse to get a percentage of the probate estate. The percentage doesn't include accounts jointly owned with someone else. A joint account owned with your daughter, for example, would go to her and not be subject to the surviving spouse's claim. The direct beneficiary of life insurance, annuities, and retirement plans are also considered non-probate assets because they pass directly to the named beneficiary and avoid the spouses' elective share. Assets held in a Living Revocable Trust are also assets that pass outside probate to the named beneficiaries. Until recently, a surviving spouse was unable to claim a spouse's elective share for assets passing via the Living Revocable Trust. Under new Florida law, F.S. 732.201, a surviving spouse now has the right to claim 30% of all assets of the estate, including life insurance cash benefits, retirement annuities, joint accounts, gifts made one year before death, and assets held in a Living Revocable Trust. This statute closes the loophole and requires a spouse to formally and knowingly waive their right to the 30% share by signing a pre-nuptial or post-nuptial agreement.*

Can he get my money?

The woman sitting across from me was very upset. “I need to know if my ex-husband can get his hands on my assets now and my estate after my death. He’s a liar and I know he’ll come after my estate. He tricked me into marrying him and then he divorced me.” She took a deep breath. “You have to help me protect my estate.”

“I understand your concerns about your ex-husband, but I don’t think he’ll be a problem. Since you are divorced, he won’t be able to get your assets now and he certainly won’t be able to make a claim on your estate. Divorce severs all marital ties. Even if you left your husband’s name in your Will, he would be omitted by law.”

She was clearly not convinced. “That doesn’t matter. I know he’ll try to find a way to get my estate. He is conniving and will do anything to get at me.”

I was beginning to think she was a little obsessed or this guy was a real wacko. No matter what I said she still kept shaking her head saying, “I just know he’s going to get my money.”

Finally I said, “What is your ex-husband doing now?”

“He and his new wife and their kids live in Ohio.”

“He’s married?” I said incredulously. “How long?”

She thought for a moment. “I think about fourteen years.”

“How long have you been divorced?”

“We got divorced in 1984, so it’s been seventeen years.”

I was stunned. “You’ve been divorced for seventeen years and you’re still concerned about him taking things from you?” She nodded. “Let me see if I have this right. You’ve been divorced for seventeen years; he’s been remarried for fourteen years and now has a new family.”

“That’s right.”

"What makes you think he wants anything from you?"

"I know how he thinks," she said grimly. "He wants to get my money and whatever he can get from my estate."

"Don't you think its time for you to get over this guy?" I said gently. "After all, he has certainly moved on with his life."

She didn't answer, just crossed her arms and shook her head. It was obvious there was no hope for this lady. She was truly obsessed. I tried to explain that her assets were not at risk, but I made no progress whatsoever. In the end, I performed no legal services for her and she left my office dissatisfied. I never saw her again.

> ***Legal Analysis:*** *Divorce severs all legal ties regarding estates. However, there are several interesting legal oddities. Regardless what assets you left your wife in your Will, she is automatically out once the divorce is final because she is no longer your wife. However, if she is a named beneficiary on your life insurance policy, she would still get the death benefits because divorce does not terminate her rights as the named beneficiary. This is true for the beneficiary designations on virtually all other assets such as IRAs, 401(k)s, and annuities.*

Neighbor, take my wife...please

After the gentleman seated himself, I asked him "How can I help you?"

"I'm not really into all this estate-planning stuff, he began. I'm only doing it for my wife, but I want everything tied up in a Trust. I've talked to my neighbor who's also a friend of mine, and he's agreed to be the Trustee and take care of my wife's financial needs if I die."

I was shocked. "You mean your neighbor—some guy—is going pay all of your wife's bills for the rest of her life and give her a monthly allowance with her own money?"

He looked puzzled. "Of course. What's wrong with that?"

"I think it's a little...unusual."

"You don't understand," he said impatiently. "My wife is totally incapable of handling money. This is for her own good. She's just a woman."

I asked, "Well, where is she? Why isn't she here today discussing this?"

He snorted. "She wouldn't understand any of this. I want to set things up so that she'll be taken care of. I don't want her to have to worry about anything and I don't want any scam artists taking advantage of her."

I looked at him. "What makes you think your neighbor won't take advantage of her?"

He waved off my concerns. "I know I can trust him."

I shook my head. "In my opinion, the selection of your neighbor is a problem waiting to happen. What if he gets sick, becomes an alcoholic, or develops Alzheimer's? Also, I have a real problem with your wife not being here at this meeting to discuss something that will affect the rest of her life. If she agrees, why not select a bank or brokerage Trust department to help manage her affairs? They are bonded professionals who will always be there and will look after your wife's best interest."

I explained more about how Trust departments worked, but I could tell he was not impressed with my advice. He sat there with his arms folded, tuning me out. He wanted to do it his way. We discussed several other small matters and then he left. He never came back. Maybe he found another lawyer to do his bidding, but I don't think so. I suspect he's done nothing and he's just going to leave a big mess for his unprepared wife. Even so, in this case, I think doing nothing is better than having the neighbor in charge. Painful though it may be, she will learn, as many sheltered women have before her, how to do things on her own.

One of the best gifts a man can give his wife is financial knowledge and experience. If she has never handled the bills before, he should turn over the checkbook and investments to her for at least two months. She will struggle with the accounting and financial decisions, but he can help guide her and answer questions. Otherwise, if the husband dies and she has no experience, she can be overwhelmed with financial worries at a time when she is also dealing with the grief of losing a husband.

In my opinion, the successful estate plan removes this uncertainty at a time when there are more pressing concerns. Dealing with doctors, end of life decisions, death, burial, and family should be the top priority. Wondering how the bills will get paid should not be a concern.

Legal Analysis: *There is no law that protects a wife in the above scenario. Sometimes a wife will sign away the rights she has at her husband's request. Once all of the assets are set up in a Trust, there may be few ways to unlock the Trust. Sometimes, the only way a wife can protect herself is to file for divorce and get half of the assets. Once the husband dies, if no prior action was taken, the assets are locked up in the Trust and divorce (obviously) is no longer an option.*

Epilog: *The husband did die unexpectedly. He had done nothing for his wife as I suspected. In this instance, doing nothing was the best decision. She now has remodeled the house and is spending some money. However, had he saddled her with an irrevocable trust, with a neighbor as trustee, her life would have been very complicated. I have met her on several occasions and found her to be very intelligent and feel she will be successful managing her assets.*

I'm buying my child's inheritance

There are those who live for their children. One recent client was just such a person. I met with her to review and update her estate documents and she was very insistent that all her assets pass to her two children after her death. She said she had lost her husband ten years ago and he didn't leave the family with any security. His insurance, through work, was only one and a half times his salary and he had only a small retirement account.

She took his insurance proceeds, along with the money she made at her job, and used it for her kids. "They lacked for nothing," she told me. "I helped pay for their college and I helped them with the down payments for their cars. It has taken every penny I have to help support my kids and give them a good education, and if I had more I would give it to them." Then she started to cry. "The one regret I now have is that I won't be able to leave them any inheritance."

"Why is this so important to you?" I asked.

She looked at me with a tear-stained face and said, "I got nothing from my parents when they died. They didn't love me enough to leave me anything. I had to pay for their burial out of my own pocket and I even paid for the last utility bill for the house they were renting. I love my children and would never do that to them. I want them to know I truly love them and I don't want them to have to pay to bury me. I want them to have an inheritance, something special from me when I die, even if I die in a sudden car accident."

I prepared a Will, Power of Attorney, Health Care Surrogate, and Living Will for her. Her children were named in the appropriate places and would have no problems when handling the estate. We then turned to the inheritance issue. She told me she worked as a secretary for a local business. She liked her job and felt she was fairly compensated for someone with just a high school education. I suggested she could go back to school, get a college education and change jobs to make more money. She said, "I love my job and I'm happy where I am now."

“Well,” I offered, “unless you marry a rich guy or win the lottery, you’ll probably never have a large estate.”

She agreed, “The problem is, I don’t want to remarry and I don’t play the lottery.” We discussed investing, but she told me her risk tolerance was limited to CDs.

I next suggested if she was intent on leaving an inheritance, she consider buying an insurance policy. I said, “If you buy a life insurance policy, it will provide your children with the inheritance you want to give them. You pay a monthly premium. It’s like an investment. However, if something should happen to you now or in the next couple of years, your children will get that inheritance.” She liked the idea since it fit her monthly budget. She purchased a $250,000 level premium term policy that endows at age ninety-nine. If she dies before she reaches ninety-nine, the children get the insurance proceeds. If she lives to age ninety-nine, the policy endows and the insurance company pays the $250,000 directly to her. Either way, her kids are assured an inheritance unless she stops making her monthly premium payments. She also paid for an additional rider (until age 65) that pays her monthly premium if she should suffer a disability and lose her job.

In the world today, there are as many people alive over the age 65 as in all previous history put together.

Are we getting divorced?

When Trust documents are signed, it is a formal and paper-intensive affair. Many clients say, "This is like a real estate closing." They have a point. The Trust signing usually involves one hundred to one hundred and fifty pages of documents. The average couple will sign two Wills, two Trusts, two Powers of Attorney, two Health Care Surrogates, two Living Wills, several deeds, a Trust Summary, and bank and broker notifications. As I review the documents one at a time with my clients, we discuss and look at each document, and I ask if they have any questions. If there are no questions, I flip through each document and date-stamp each one. I then remove the individual documents from the Trust book and place them in a neat pile for signing. The number of documents circulating the conference table can be very intimidating.

During one of the signing conferences, a couple in a second marriage was busy signing their various Trust documents. The husband was leaving nearly everything to his wife and very little to his children by his first marriage. They had not been married that long and she was clearly nervous. After signing about half of the documents, she suddenly sat up straight, and with an anxious look on her face asked, "These aren't divorce papers, are they?"

My son, the grandson

In this next case, I'd like to brag that I gave my client great advice, but it was really his idea and done before I met him. This particular gentleman had reared several children. One daughter had mental problems and was in and out of jail and treatment facilities. Somewhere along the way, she gave birth to a son. She was unable to properly care for him, so the boy lived with her dad (my client). The father of the child had little or no contact with the boy and was constantly in arrears with his child support payments.

My client supported his grandson and made most of the child rearing decisions, but he had no legal authority over his grandson. Over time, the mother's mental problems worsened until, eventually, she was placed in a mental facility, leaving the boy without a legal guardian. His father was not an option. He was a street bum, neither willing nor able to help. The child required normal medical and dental care. He needed school clothes, school supplies, and all the other things any young boy should have. Neither the boy's mother nor father could supply any of the needed items. After the boy's mother was placed in a treatment facility, my client, the grandfather, initiated legal action to adopt this boy, his grandson, as his own son. The mother and father both agreed that this adoption was in their son's best interest. The biological father quickly agreed, glad to be free of the legal obligation including child support payments. The parents signed the legal papers and the judge executed the order for the adoption. The boy was now legally the son of his grandfather. This was significant for several reasons. First, my client now had total legal custody of the boy. The boy couldn't be taken in the middle of the night by the parents. My client would be able to make all decisions regarding the rearing of this boy. My client was a retired military officer, so the boy now had Base privileges, as would any military dependent. He can now shop on Base, see Base doctors, or be treated under Tricare, the military health insurance program. Since the boy was a minor, he was entitled to receive certain death benefits and social security payments, if my client died before the boy reached the age of eighteen. All of these benefits are now available to this boy because he was adopted by a loving, caring grandfather, willing to take on the responsibility of raising another child late in life.

Legal Analysis: *In order to adopt, you must have the permission of both biological parents. If the child is not adopted, but cared for by the grandparent, the problems are immense. Who is responsible for medical bills? Who will take him to the hospital and make healthcare decisions? What can you do if the parents show up on your doorstep in the middle of the night and want to take their child? You don't have a legal right to object. The law makes no distinctions between a biological child and an adopted child. An adopted child and all of the adopted child's issue (children) are now part of your lineal descendants.*

The average funeral costs a little more than $6,000. About $2,300 of this expense is for the casket.

Her tears

We all remember certain conversations or events as vividly as if they had happened just moments ago. The JFK assassination, the "Challenger" disaster and the World Trade Center destruction are several that come to mind. As an estate-planning attorney, certain professional situations are just as vivid to me. Take, for instance, an afternoon meeting with a client that will always be burned into my memory.

I was meeting with an elderly lady who had never been married. She was a retired Air Force officer, now in her seventies, who had worked hard to be successful in the male dominated military. She was understandably proud of her accomplishments and I was impressed. When we got around to discussing certain aspects of estate planning, she seemed to struggle a bit with some of my questions, especially when I asked, "If you were unable to make healthcare or financial decisions for yourself, who would make them for you?"

Eyes downcast, she didn't say anything for several minutes as she thought over my question. Finally she looked up at me and I saw tears in her eyes. "I have no one," she admitted. "I don't know who I could rely on."

I felt a pang in my heart as we both realized she was totally alone and there would be no one there for her if the need arose. I still remember how she looked, sitting there in my office, tears trickling down the crease in her cheek. I don't know what happened to her. She never came back to complete her estate planning.

After this meeting it dawned on me why I (and millions of other parents) go through the hell of raising children. Unlike this retired officer, when I'm old, at least I'll have someone to take care of me.

Legal Analysis: *If no one is available to care for someone, the state takes over through the Department of Children and Families. They will establish a guardianship so that legal and healthcare decisions can be made. A family member who petitions for guardianship may or may not be selected to be the guardian. The* *court will determine who will best serve the interest of the ward. A durable power of attorney, healthcare surrogate, and possibly a Living Revocable Trust are documents needed so that the courts are not involved. Remember, estate planning is like ordering from a menu—you get to make the selections. If you don't make them, the courts will.*

In today's society, children do not mature as fast as they did in our grandparents generation. Most of my clients, when they were 19, lived outside of the home, were married and fighting in a war. Now, this same maturity level is not reached until age 29 or so. I think there has been a 10 year shift of maturity levels.

We were married. Why does his Mom get the money?

There are several quirks in the law. One deals with insurance policies and other assets controlled by beneficiary designations such as insurance death benefits, annuity payments, and Payable on Death (POD) clauses.

A very young widow, in tears, was sitting in my office across from my desk. She said she had just lost her husband.

"[Andrew] died in a car accident two months ago," she said tremblingly.

I raised my eyebrows and said sincerely, "I'm very sorry for your loss."

"He was coming home from work, late, in his truck. He ran off the road and hit a tree. I'm not sure what happened. He may have fallen asleep or whatever. I don't know. He's dead. We've been married for about six months. Our baby's due next month." She paused a minute to steady herself, and then continued, "Andrew's never going to see his son. The reason I'm here is because we didn't have any money. Oh, I think there was $281.00 dollars in our checking account. The only asset of value he had was a life insurance policy for $25,000. He had it before he met me. I think his mom talked him into getting it. He paid the premium every month. I remember seeing the checks go out of our account. I always had the steady job. Sometimes he was out of work. I think I paid for more of the premiums than he did. Well, anyway, the problem is that the beneficiary on the life insurance policy was his mother. She was the beneficiary before we got married. I know he wanted me to be the beneficiary. He was so happy about being a father. I know he would want our son to have this money. But unfortunately, he never got around to changing the beneficiary before he died."

"Are you telling me he died with no assets and one insurance policy payable to his mother?"

"Isn't there some law that protects me in a situation like this?"

"I'm afraid not. The beneficiary designation controls where the insurance proceeds go after death. A Will does not control this money if the beneficiary designation has been selected. If the insurance had been left to his estate, then the Will controls where the money goes. You don't get to claim the insurance just because you're married to him."

"My mother-in-law said I couldn't get any of the insurance money. She and I have never got along. I'm not sure she believes this child belongs to her son."

"Well, does it?"

"I'm pretty sure it does," she responded, unconvincingly.

Legal Analysis: *Florida's Spousal Elective Share statute gives the spouse a right to claim 30% of the cash value of a life insurance policy. However, this insurance had no cash value. Therefore, the entire amount went to the mother-in-law. This new law supersedes the beneficiary designation of all financial instruments but only to the extent of 30% of the total estate assets. Otherwise, the beneficiary designation controls in all other situations. Most states do not have this new spousal protective law.*

The black sheep son

An elderly couple in their seventies had three sons. One son was the proverbial 'black sheep' with all of the accompanying felony arrests and tattoos. The couple was understandably unhappy with this one wayward child. He had disappointed them on so many occasions. They spent countless thousands of dollars bailing him out—literally, from numerous problems.

Their estate consisted of CDs and Money Market Funds. They were renting an apartment. They decided to sign a new Will changing the previous estate distribution. The estate had always been divided in three equal shares. However, since this one son had been such a disappointment, they now wanted the two good sons to get all of the estate assets, and they wanted this 'bad' son to get nothing. They softened a bit after reflection. Their assets totaled to a little more than $300,000. They decided not to exclude this one son completely, so they left him a bequest of only $20,000. The remaining balance of their estate would be divided into two equal shares. Based upon current market values, the wayward son would get $20,000 and the two good sons would get $140,000 each.

Time takes its toll on certain estates. In this case, the couple suffered several major illnesses. They used their money to pay for doctor visits and medications. Ten years later, both Mom and Dad are gone and the remaining assets consisted of one CD worth about $20,000. The rest was spent on living expenses and medical bills. During this ten year period, when the parents needed the care and comfort of their children, the black sheep son never visited or even made a phone call to check on them. He was a no-show at both funerals.

The Will directed a bequest to this black-sheep son in the amount of $20,000. A bequest is always paid first before the 'remainder beneficiaries' get their money. In this case, because the proper estate planning had not been done, the 'black sheep' son got his $20,000 bequest and the two good, loving, attentive sons got nothing.

Legal Analysis: *Bequests are paid first, free of estate tax unless there are no other assets with which to pay estate taxes. Bequests are paid before the residuary beneficiaries are paid. This can be very devastating to an estate if the proper estate planning hasn't been done. The parents could have designated the son to get 6.6% of the estate. This would have equaled $20,000 of the $300,000 estate. If the estate value ended up at $20,000.00, like it did in this case, the Black Sheep son would have gotten $1,333.33 ($20,000 x 6.6% = $1,333.33). The use of the percentage method would have protected the residuary beneficiaries from this tragedy. Sometimes it's just easier to give a set dollar amount and be rid of the problem. If the amounts are nominal (say, $5000 to $10,000) then a bequest of that amount is appropriate. This keeps the problem child from maintaining an interest in the estate proceedings. He could contest the final accounting claiming it was faulty. He could drag the proceedings out for years. If he got a dollar amount, a check could be cut and his involvement would be terminated, thereby allowing the estate proceedings to terminate quickly and efficiently.*

My son married an older woman

The woman sat with tears glistening in her eyes, looked at me and said, "I don't want to leave my son any of my estate."

"Okay," I replied. "It's your estate. You can do whatever you want with your own assets. You don't have to leave your money to your son if you would prefer not to. You don't have to leave him one dollar or any other minimal amount. All you must do is acknowledge him and direct that he will receive nothing."

She began to sob and blurted angrily, "That woman took my son from me. She's 18 years older than him. Why should I leave any of my estate to my son? She'll just take it from him."

"Have you had problems with her?" I asked.

"No. I've never talked to her."

"You may find that she's a very nice person if you get to know her," I offered.

She stared at me in amazement. "That woman will never set foot in my house," she hissed, "NEVER!"

I tried to discuss the issue with her but made absolutely no progress. Her mind was made up and her feelings might as well have been cast in stone. As far as she was concerned, this older woman had taken her most valuable possession and for that, she would never forgive her. I told her that because of her obstinacy she might well lose her son too.

She looked at me as tears coursed down her cheeks. "Mister Fisher," she whispered. "I've already lost my son."

Although I advised against it, she insisted I draw up a Will, which excluded her son. When I was convinced there was no changing her mind, that is what I did.

Legal Analysis: *There is no requirement that an omission from a Will be based upon a reasonable standard. You may omit a beneficiary for any reason. That includes reasons that may not be acceptable in other areas of the law (i.e., race, creed, age, sex, marriage). As an example, one of my clients wanted only the male heirs to inherit the assets of his estate. When I questioned him about the exclusion of his granddaughters, he said, "They can get married and have a husband take care of them. The boys will have to support a family. They'll need the money."*

In my opinion, a child under the age of 25 should never receive a large lump sum of money. They do not appreciate the money and do not have the discipline to keep it. Most will squander it in the first few years and never have it as security for retirement.

She's wonderful

"I have one child, but I feel as though I have two," my client said. "My son married the most wonderful girl. I talk to her almost every day and she is the most wonderful person I have ever known. My son is very lucky to have her. She is really something wonderful."

"I would say she sounds…wonderful," I said, smiling.

"Oh, she is," he said. "She definitely is."

I glanced at my notes. "I understand you want to leave everything to your son if living and, if not, then to your grandson. Is that right?"

He was shaking his head, "No, I want to leave one-half of my estate to my son and one-half to my daughter-in-law."

"That's not what's normally done. Most people leave their estates to their children if living and, if not, then to their grandchildren. When you look at a Will it has those Latin words, 'per stirpes.' That means 'by the root.' Your estate is passed on down the bloodline. If you left one-half of your estate to your daughter-in-law, she could divorce him and still get one-half of your estate. If she remarried, her new husband could get all the money you gave her."

He was smiling. "You don't understand. My daughter-in-law is more of a daughter to me than my son is a son. If they got divorced, I wouldn't care. I still want her to get one-half of my estate. She's just wonderful."

Legal Analysis: *The normal way an estate passes is "per stirpes" or down the blood-line. This means, if your child is living, he gets the share. If he is not living, then it does not go to his wife, it goes further down the blood-line to the grandchildren, and so on. Spouses are never included, unless, like my client in the above example, it is done intentionally.*

There is one way a spouse gets the estate assets. If, at the death of the father, the son is living, he gets all of the estate assets as stipulated in his father's Will. However, if the son dies a year later, all of his estate assets, including the inherited money, passes to his wife via his Will. Not much can be done about that situation unless the estate assets are held in Trust for the rest of the son's life. Then at the son's death, the estate assets can pass directly to the grandchildren. The Trust created to hold the assets must be managed by an independent Trustee who receives a yearly Trustee fee. The son will have no right to get to the principal to use as he wishes. I discourage this type of planning unless there is an overriding reason—like alcoholism, drug addiction, or mental instability—to deny a child his full inheritance. Of course, if the estate is greater than say, $50 million, then there would be a desire to spread that amount over more than one generation.

Mom liked me best

In this case, the mother purchased a home for herself and her daughter, titling the home in the name of the daughter. Mom also purchased the daughter a nice car, even though the daughter had more assets than Mom. These gifts were motivated by love—they shared a house and their lives. The daughter gave up her independence but got to spend special time with her mother. This relationship lasted for ten years. During this time, Mom was very generous with her other child. She gave $11,000 a year to her other daughter, her husband and their children.

When Mom died, she left a Trust which divided the estate in two equal shares. However, the two large gifts—the house and the car—were made prior to death. Under the law, there is a presumption that these gifts were made free of any estate tax consideration unless a contrary intention is expressed in the Trust or Will. Further, these gifts were made with a presumption that they were not advancements on an inheritance. When the 706 Estate Tax return was completed, the CPA had to file 709 gift tax returns for the prior years in which the large gifts were made. The 709s placed the IRS on notice that the Mom's Unified Credit was being used to make these gifts. While there was no gift tax due on these transfers, the transfers did use part of her lifetime credit. The credit, at the time of her death, was $1,500,000. Unfortunately, the prior gifts used $500,000 of her credit. This meant the unified credit of $1,500,000 was reduced by $500,000, leaving $1,000,000 available at her death.

Her estate, at death, was valued around 1.5 million dollars, which meant $500,000 was exposed to inheritance taxes. The balance of the estate after Mom's death was used to pay the inheritance taxes. The house and car were gifts received by the daughter, inheritance tax free. This meant both daughters must bear the burden of paying the inheritance taxes. Not surprisingly, the daughter who had to pay taxes on the house and car she did not receive was not pleased.

Legal Analysis: *Florida has resolved some of these thorny tax problems by enacting a statute that requires the tax burden to be shared among all beneficiaries rather than just the residuary* *beneficiaries. However, prior gifts are still not included. If a parent gives a $500,000 gift prior to death, the recipient is not responsible for estate or gift taxes. Any taxes due must be paid when the remaining estate is ready for distribution. The gift is added back into the estate, to be taxed. In essence, the residuary heirs contribute tax dollars to a gift they did not receive.*

One final note: the 2001 Tax Act increased the amount that can be passed to heirs tax-free. In 2004, this amount was $1,500,000. In 2006, this amount increases to $2,000,000. Check with your CPA or Estate Attorney for the current amount.

Some clients own property in foreign countries. I advise them to place such property in joint ownership with their children to avoid probate in the U.S. and the foreign country.

Show me the money!

Sometimes I have more than one client from the same family. In one situation, the grandfather saw me first and then I saw his two children. One child had no children and the other only one son—the only grandson. The grandfather was dividing his estate among his two sons—and his grandson. One son and his wife were leaving their estate to their son (the grandson). The other son and his wife with no children were likewise leaving their estate to the only heir, their nephew (the grandson). That meant that, in the event of a major tragedy, all the assets of this family, about five million dollars, could suddenly end up in the hands of this grandson. The grandson is 30 years old with a GED high school diploma, working part-time as a handyman. He lives in a house owned by his grandfather and pays no rent. He is a bum.

"He's just the nicest boy you would ever want to meet," the grandfather offered. Then he looked around the office as if to make sure we were the only ones there, and said, "He hasn't done much with his life and sometimes he isn't very trustworthy. But he is my only grandchild." He closed his eyes and shook his head. "Other than my children, he's the only heir I have. He is eventually going to get everything."

The other family members were concerned at the idea of this son/grandson/nephew receiving such a large estate. They weren't at all sure he was capable of handling the money or even holding on to it. I suggested they do the following: present him with a $10,000 check and say he can cash it only after he completes a finance class, at the local university, with a grade of B or better. After that class, other classes would be offered with an accompanying cash payment. My thinking was that since he is going to get the money eventually, why not educate him with his own money now? Why not give him a financial test drive? If he fails the classes or uses the money unwisely, then a significant change in the estate plan should be considered. One option might be to establish a Trust to dole out the inheritance on a monthly basis for the rest of his life.

Legal Analysis: *The family options include giving all of the money to the grandson immediately, doling it out over time, or giving it in periodic lump sum payments. They could also choose to leave the child out altogether. Most folks seem to have an overriding desire to leave their children, grandchildren, or other heirs their money. While they certainly don't want the money to destroy the life of a child, this is precisely what can happen. My experience shows that most inheritances will be spent within 10 years after receipt. Look how the lottery winners fare. About 75% of all lottery winners are broke after 10 years or after the last lottery payment has been made. In my opinion, the way a family can make a financial difference in the life of a young (and perhaps irresponsible) heir is to not give them all their inheritance at once. Tie it up in Trust until the heir reaches a certain age, perhaps 40 or 50. By then they will have lived a good part of their life, they will be more settled and a large influx of cash will not derail them. When an hourly worker inherits several hundred thousand dollars it's unlikely they will keep taking crap from a boss who now has less money than they do.*

It's amazing how much smarter you think you are when you have a lot of money. It's even more amazing how much smarter others think you are because you have a lot of money—even if you didn't do anything to get it other than being born. The problems start when you have not developed the discipline to keep it. Believe me, it will be gone in fewer than 10 years, unless you get the money at a time in your life when you are more settled, perhaps around age 50 or so. You may go on a trip, buy a computer, or get new tires for the car, but you are not likely to change careers or tell your boss to "take this job and shove it." You may choose to retire early, take the trips and enjoy life, with no financial worries. The downside occurs when the intended heir dies before enjoying any of the money. If your irresponsible child doesn't make it to 50, at least the money will still be there for the grandchildren or other designated heirs.

The second marriage — life goes on (even without you)

Twenty-five to thirty-five percent of my practice involves couples in their second or subsequent marriage. Even though a spouse dies or a divorce occurs, life for the remaining spouse goes on and there can be numerous problems. Often the surviving spouse meets someone new or rekindles an old relationship. Before the new couple gets married, the savvy ones see me first so I can draft a Living Revocable Trust and a Pre-Nuptial Agreement. They get their affairs in order and the husband and wife keep their assets separate, making arrangements for their respective estates to be distributed to their own children. Most don't need each other's money to live.

Of course, not all couples have done proper estate planning and are this financially secure. Most have made no plans and commonly, they need their deceased spouse's assets to maintain a comfortable lifestyle. They visit me expecting a simple solution, but this problem can be difficult to resolve. A couple with a modest estate ($100,000 to $500,000) usually has the house and all other assets titled jointly. If not jointly titled, their Wills usually leave all assets to each other and then to their children. Often they think the Will of the first to die has some legal power upon the death of the second spouse, but it doesn't.

If all marital assets are jointly titled, then upon the death of the first spouse they immediately belong to the surviving spouse. There is no probate. Since a Will only has legal authority in probate court, the deceased spouse's Will has no effect. The surviving spouse owns, outright, all of the jointly titled assets and thus the surviving spouse's Will controls where the assets go after death.

The couple will sit in my office and look at each other and one will say, "Oh honey, you know you can trust me. I will take care of your children." But there are many problems with this scenario. Consider the husband upon his remarriage. Why would he want to take care of a deceased spouse's children when he now has a new wife to look after? She's the one who needs the security. Most men don't leave assets to their own children after remarriage (more on this later) so why would they leave it to the children of a deceased spouse?

I offer several solutions to clients faced with this dilemma. If the assets are sufficient, for example, $1 million owned by each client, they can keep their estates divided and direct their separate shares go to their respective families. If the estate is not that large and all assets are needed by the surviving spouse, the couple can purchase life insurance to provide an inheritance to the children of the first to die. This will be all they get because the surviving spouse keeps all other assets.

Most men have insurance while few women do. Even with younger couples, the guys have higher limits.

Our children are bums but there may be hope for the grandchildren

Many clients complain about the financial decisions made by their children. Routinely, I hear "The children are just fine, but they sure do spend a lot of money." One couple, fed up with their children's financial shenanigans, asked me to change their Trust document.

The husband was exasperated. "My son has a new Mercedes Benz. It's the big one. I have always wanted one like that."

He stared at me for a minute and then said, "We're wondering how in the world he can afford to make the payments. I know he owes almost $20,000 in credit card debt. It just galls me to know he and his wife are paying twenty percent interest. There ought to be a law to keep the interest rates down on those credit cards. It seems like they give those cards to the most irresponsible people. And then the companies complain when the debt gets charged off in bankruptcy."

He shook his head. "I don't know how they can even pay their bills."

Up until now the wife had been sitting quietly, but she suddenly sat up straight and said acidly, "They can pay their bills because you keep sending them money!"

I know, I know," he admitted, "but what can I do? I don't want them to lose everything or end up in jail because of bad checks."

I said, "I agree with you that something should be done, but in my opinion, you're not doing them any favors by constantly bailing them out with your money. The best gift you can give is one of financial training and independence."

The husband shook his head, "No, no, we're way beyond that. I admit we made mistakes in how we raised our children, but I'm not sure where we went wrong teaching them financial responsibility. It doesn't seem that hard to understand. You can't spend money if you don't have it. If you keep borrowing to pay for 'things,' you'll soon owe more than you earn." He sighed, "But our children don't seem to understand this."

He took a deep breath. "So we're giving up on them." His wife was nodding her head in agreement. "Any inheritance they get from us will just be squandered. It'll do more harm than good. We've decided to skip our children and transfer our assets directly to an educational Trust for our grandchildren."

His wife said, "We think if we educate the grandchildren, they will turn out better and be more responsible than our children did."

Legal Analysis: *You are not obligated to leave your assets to your children. You made the money and you can do with it as you please. You can leave it all to them, you can leave some to them, or you can leave them nothing. Many clients have set up educational Trusts for grandchildren. Most carve off a portion of the estate assets and use that money to establish the educational Trust. Some clients feel if their son, for example, got the entire inheritance he would just blow it and not use it to educate the grandchildren. In that case, a client could allocate half of the son's share to the grandchild's educational Trust and half to the son. It could be a fixed dollar amount or a percentage of the estate.*

In my experience, the average amount of money placed in the educational Trust is between $20,000 and $150,000. The terms of the Trust allow for the funds to be used for any type of education—preschool, primary, secondary, college, post graduate, vocational, or personal enhancement. The Trustee has the latitude to pay for all reasonable and necessary educational expenses. Such expenses include, but are not limited to: tuition, room and board, books, fees, meals, transportation expenses; even spending money. The safety net language allows the Trustee to distribute the Trust assets if, in the Trustee's discretion, it is determined it would be in the best interest of the beneficiary to receive the funds immediately.

Usually I include a distribution age of 30. When the grandchild reaches the age of 30 he or she gets the assets held in their edu-

cational Trust. In my opinion, this fosters a more judicious management of the Trust assets. A grandchild will be more likely to seek a grant or scholarship if they know they get what's left in the educational Trust at age 30. There is no incentive to "use it or lose it."

Some clients want this educational Trust to provide educational funds for several generations. This is now possible in Florida given the recent legislative change regarding the Rule against Perpetuities (F.S. 689.225). Before the change, the Rule against Perpetuities prevented Trusts from providing unlimited generational educational funds. Under the new law, a Florida Trust can last as long as 360 years. Other states have completely eliminated the rule against perpetuities and it is possible to create an educational Trust that lasts almost forever.

"If there is a will … I want to be in it!"

"If there is a will … there is a wait."

House husband

The couple looked like most other couples I had met with over the years, but with a decided difference. The wife was a full Colonel in the Air Force and clearly the dominant voice in the meeting. Apparently the husband didn't have a permanent job. She was the breadwinner; he moved around the country with her as she was transferred. He was a "house husband" and stayed home and took care of the children. After we discussed various estate planning issues, we got to the point where a successor Trustee was to be selected. She suggested that she be the Trustee now and if she died before her husband, he should have a co-Trustee to act with him.

She placed her hand over the side of her face nearest to her husband so as to block his view of her lips and whispered to me, "He doesn't really understand finances."

Through all this he just sat there looking blankly at the wall, pretending not to listen. There is a first time for everything and this was the first time I found a wife as the dominant spouse and the husband treated like the helpless weaker partner.

Legal Comment: *Since the sixties, more and more women have maintained permanent jobs. Indeed, more women are enrolled in medical school than men. As a result, many more husbands are taking the role of primary housekeeper and childrearer. Question: Does raising children reduce one's financial abilities?*

A mother's love

A mother's love is true and deep and hard to weaken. However, there are circumstances and events even the most devoted mothers can't ignore. For instance, a client of mine has a daughter with an addictive personality. She was addicted to boys and cigarettes at a young age and by the time she was fifteen she was pregnant and smoking two packs of cigarettes a day. A year later she graduated to crack cocaine and sex for money and was in and out of juvenile detention centers until she reached her 18th birthday. Shortly thereafter she was convicted as an adult and spent time in a real jail. Along the way, my client hired, at one time or another, most of the psychologists and counselors in town, but soon gave up, since none offered any real hope or solutions. "No one can help this child unless she wants to help herself," they said.

Eighteen years later, at age 36, this daughter is still in and out of jail. Each time she is released, Mom holds her breath and hopes and prays this time will be different. Unfortunately, Mom doesn't get to hold her breath very long. She usually receives a call from the police station within a few days following release to notify her that her daughter has fallen back into the gutter. After twenty years of frustration, Mom decided she would no longer pay for her daughter's legal bills or support her in any way. Mom has been disappointed so many times that she has lost all respect for her daughter, but she has not lost her motherly love. It's been my experience that—as a general rule—women feel responsible for their children. If the child turns out badly, many mothers feel it was their fault. Men, on the other hand, routinely say "to hell with them. They've made their own decisions and now they must live with them." Men generally don't feel the self-guilt a woman does.

My client related to me the countless lies, the expenses, and her deep disappointment with her daughter, who was currently in prison, serving time for a drug conviction. In my office to discuss estate planning, Mom said, "I'm not sure what to leave my daughter in my Will."

I could hardly believe my ears. "Why would you leave her anything?"

"Well," she said, "she is my daughter."

“I understand, and it is your money, so you can leave it to anyone you wish, but this money will not benefit your daughter. In fact, it could hasten her death. She’ll probably use it to throw the biggest crack party in the county.”

She nodded. “I know, but she is my daughter and I feel bad for the way her life has turned out. I want to leave her something.”

I sighed. “I can make sure she gets a monthly check for the rest of her life, but knowing your daughter’s past history, are you sure you want to do that?”

Tears glistened in her eyes as she said, “I know I shouldn’t do it, but I have to.”

Following her instructions, I drafted a Trust agreement that would hold all her assets in Trust, but still provide the daughter with a monthly stipend for the rest of her life, whether she was in jail or not. I suggested a drug test before each payment but Mom would not agree. She knew her daughter would never be clean. By no stretch of the imagination could this woman be considered a devoted, loving, and dutiful daughter. It was only the mother’s guilt that drove her to leave her daughter money. My client was involved with many local charities and she could have made a great financial impact by giving them her money.

Even though I didn’t agree with my client’s decision, my job is to advise and describe options to my clients without making decisions for them. I try not to influence my clients to the point where they are not exercising their own free will and try to make sure they leave my office knowing they made their own decisions. In this case, my client wanted a lifetime Trust payment for her daughter. If this daughter survived to the age of 62, she would probably have no retirement or social security. However, she will have this lifetime trust payment. It won’t make her rich, but it will be enough to pay for a modest apartment and a bag or two of groceries. If she is in jail, then she will have spending money for cigarettes and candy bars.

Legal Analysis: *Children who are drug addicts or alcoholics have no ability to handle money. For them to receive a large inheritance (more than a few thousand dollars) would generally* *do more harm than good. Some clients fear for the life of their child if such a large cash payment were received, and with good reason. An addicted child might use all of the money to snort up a year's worth of cocaine in one week. A large influx of money could also attract the wrong "friends" who might take advantage, or steal the money outright.*

Some parents realize their child is totally incompetent in handling money. One couple told me, "If we give him money, he'll just lose it, spend it, or give it away. We know in our hearts he will not have any of this inheritance in one year." These scenarios call for the type of estate planning aptly named "ruling from the grave." I don't normally recommend this type of planning because I think most families should have the inheritance distributed to the children with no strings attached. This is usually quick, simple, and much less likely to cause litigation. However, under the "deadbeat child" scenario, there are several other options. One is to keep all the assets in Trust with an appointed trustee who can make the necessary monthly payments. If an invasion into the principal is needed for some extraordinary reason, such as a major medical expense, then the trustee has the option to provide that financial assistance. This arrangement works well in large estates with a corporate trustee such as a bank or brokerage firm Trust department. Trust departments will not usually administer a Trust if the estate is under $250,000. In this situation, a parent could select a family member, but I rarely recommend that. Why would a parent who has been struggling with a wayward child want to place this burden on one of his or her other children?

The personal representative or trustee could be instructed to purchase an annuity that would pay a fixed amount of money to the deadbeat child for the rest of his or her life. This eliminates the trustee fees as well as the trustee's long-term involvement. It makes it easier for the other children because the wayward child will get a monthly check until they die. The parent has ruled from the grave how this child will receive the inheritance.

My son, Mr. Wife

A distinguished gentleman and his wife were concerned about their son. They weren't sure he would be able to properly manage the assets left him after they died. They were discussing with me various ways to control the estate assets in a Trust established for him, but I had the feeling they weren't telling me everything.

Finally the wife said, "Well, I think we should just tell him. He is our lawyer and he needs to know."

The husband didn't look happy and grudgingly said, "This is very hard for me. I don't like talking about it."

"If it's that painful," I said, "You don't have to tell me—unless you feel it is relevant to your estate plan."

He sighed. "No, my wife is right. You need to know." He sat back, took a deep breath, and began. "My son announced his plans to get married to a gal he's been dating for several years and we were pleased he finally made the commitment to get married. We've always thought he had trouble making a commitment. We also felt he lacked fortitude, but getting married seemed to be a step in the right direction and a commitment. We were pleased with his decision, although we really didn't know his fiancée very well."

The wife chimed in, "We worried about him, but we were happy for him, too."

The husband raised his hand. "Let me finish my thoughts, dear." He went on, "We flew to California to attend the wedding. We were seated in the front pew, where the groom's parents sit. The rest of our family was there. We weren't crying or anything but it was emotional. You know how weddings can be."

"Yes, I do," I said. "I was crying at mine."

He didn't laugh and I thought I might have offended him. He gritted his teeth and clenched his jaw to the point I wondered how he could continue talking. Finally he said, "We were sitting in front and the minister said 'I now pronounce you man and wife.' Of course we thought the ceremony was over, but then he said 'the couple has a special announcement to make.' We figured they might say something about how much they loved each other or thank their parents or something like that." The wife was nodding her head in agreement. "Well, the minister put his arms around them and said 'This couple has decided to use the wife's last name and they shall be known from this day forward as Mr. and Mrs. [Jones].'"

He sighed and shook his head, reliving the moment. "The first thing I did was check my hearing aids, but they were working all right. Well, we were stunned. My heart was pounding in my chest and my blood pressure must have jumped a hundred points. It was several minutes before I could speak. I don't think I have ever been more embarrassed or ashamed in my life. What's wrong with our name? Does it embarrass him?" He folded his arms across his chest. "I think it shows his total lack of character."

He was still breathing hard and his wife patted his arm. "At one time, I didn't want to leave him any of our estate." He took a deep breath. "Obviously I've calmed down a bit, but we feel he has a problem and we don't want him to control any of his money. He'll probably just give it to his wife. If she can talk him into changing his name, she can probably take everything he has. We'd rather him get a small yearly amount from interest on the principal. Then his children can get the principal balance when they reach the age of thirty."

Legal Analysis: *Whether you agree or disagree with the father, this is yet another example of how to cut yourself out of parents' estate. It's their money and parents can do what they want with their own estate assets. There are few restrictions.*

Say what?

A Will is a legal document simply defined as "your last letter of instruction." A Will is in writing, signed in the presence of two witnesses, and has directions about what to do after death. It's this last part, "directions about what to do after death," that causes most of the problems.

A woman prepared her own Will, which contained the following instructions: "At my death, I direct that my estate be distributed to my sister and her three children." It sounds pretty straightforward, but is it? Does this mean her estate will go to her sister first and if she is not living, to her children? Does it mean one-half to her sister and one-half to her children? Does it mean each child and her sister will receive an equal share—25% to each? The directions are not clear. The Will should clearly state what is to happen and should not be ambiguous.

Another do-it-yourself Will said, "To my sister a life interest in the assets of my estate." The Will did not say what happened to the assets after her death. Do the assets go to the children of the sister or to the heirs at law of the decedent?

Legal Analysis: *In the first situation, the mother and her children could agree to sign waivers and let the mother have all of the estate assets. If one child disagreed, a probate proceeding would be initiated to determine what the Testatrix intended, but the judge would ultimately decide. As you might imagine, involving several lawyers and a judge will cost the heirs many thousands of dollars. In the second situation, the ultimate heirs who would get the property after the sister died are very distant relations of the lady who created the Will and have little contact with the family. It could be a real problem locating them and then keeping them updated as to the status of the estate assets. Every Will should be clear and unambiguous so that problems such as these are avoided.*

Where are you, Robin Hood?

I looked through the file in front of me. "Your husband died last year and you have two sons. Is that correct?"

My client, a well-dressed woman in her seventies, nodded, "Yes, I have two sons. One owns his own company and is doing quite well. But my other son is struggling. He's a part-time priest. He is such a dear."

"At your death, do you want your estate divided into equal shares, one for each son?"

She shook her head. "Oh, no, I want everything to go to John, the priest. He doesn't have anything and struggles week to week. Bobby has so much. He has a beautiful house and a nice car. You know he has his own company," she said again. "He's been such a hard worker and it's paid off for him. He doesn't need any of my money so I want my estate to go to Johnny."

I was surprised. "Are you sure you want all $900,000 to go to Johnny and nothing to Bobby? What about Bobby's children, your grandkids? Do you want to leave something to them?"

"They've got plenty of money. Johnny has never really had much. He worked various jobs and wasn't really successful and then he went into the ministry to become a priest. He's the one who needs my money, not Bobby."

"But is it fair to give it all to Johnny and nothing to Bobby? In essence, you're punishing the successful child and rewarding the unsuccessful one."

She sighed. "I know and I feel bad about it, but I've decided that's the way I want to do it."

"Well, it's your estate to do with as you please, but I recommend you at least tell Bobby that he and his family will receive nothing."

"I might tell him later," she offered, "but I think it will hurt his feelings."

My job is to explain your options. You decide what you want to do. I assume you've made your decision, so I will prepare the documents in the manner you instruct. But they are changeable, and if at a later date you decide you want to leave one-half to Bobby you can do that."

She nodded. "I'll keep that in mind."

I asked her to go home and sleep on this decision. She agreed and returned the next day, but her decision had not changed.

Legal Analysis: *This thinking is more common than one might expect. I call it the 'Robin Hood' syndrome. If you have good kids, then, in my opinion, they should be treated equally, regardless of their financial status. However, clients are still parents and many want desperately to help their children. But the fact is, some people seem destined to have little money. In a case like this, the successful child will wonder what he did to deserve being left out of the estate. It almost guarantees your children will hate each other or have ill feelings after you're gone, unless you explain your actions.*

Don't touch that Will

An elderly widow lived in a small peaceful town. She was now settled in her life after a very traumatic period involving her daughter. This widow lost her husband two years after the birth of their only child, sweet little Lucy. She went back to work at the factory to support and rear Lucy. Lucy attended the local public school and did quite well until she reached the 7th grade. When she turned twelve, the hormones must have kicked in because bad things started to happen. At first it was little lies. "I've done all of my homework." Then items in the house started to disappear—coins, cash, and jewelry. Lucy's circle of friends changed. No more friends with hair ribbons. They were replaced with spiked choke collars and black lipstick. Even though the widow tried to keep her daughter from dating, an older boy coaxed Lucy out of the house late one night. At age thirteen, Lucy was pregnant. The baby self-aborted after six weeks and the widow thought things would finally get back to the way they were before boys. Not so. Lucy had tasted excitement and wasn't about to let go.

Over the next three years, Lucy had many quick romances with other boys and became pregnant several other times (none born). She was arrested for marijuana possession when she was fifteen. At sixteen, she dropped out of school, loaded her meager possessions on the rear of a Harley owned by a big hairy guy, and rode away. Every year when Lucy needed a place to crash and dry out, she came back to her mother's house. She came without an invitation. She stole her mother's appliances and jewelry and pawned them at the local pawnshop. The widow would buy her things back after Lucy left town. After several trips to the pawnbroker, the widow and the broker worked out an arrangement. He offered Lucy the bottom dollar so it wouldn't cost the widow so much to buy back her own things.

These visits became more traumatic for the widow as the years passed. Lucy would blow into town and stay just long enough to steal some things, pawn them, and then leave. Sometimes Lucy's boyfriends would stay as well. The widow just couldn't call the police on her daughter. She felt guilty, as most moms do, with a child like this. Deep down she felt there was something she did or didn't do that caused Lucy to be this way. "Surely, a daughter couldn't be this way on her own. It must have been caused by something I did," she reflected.

One visit was particularly brutal for the widow. Lucy and her guy friend were drinking and doing some kind of drugs. She later told the police she wasn't sure what that white powder was. After a round of dancing and virtually destroying the living room furniture, the widow couldn't restrain herself any longer. She told her daughter to stop destroying the house and leave immediately. Lucy flew into a rage and hit her mother several times in the face. The widow filed a police report and the officer issued a peace bond requiring Lucy to stay away from her mother. But Lucy continued making her occasional visits, and the widow silently endured the torture. The widow never called the police. After 20 long years, the widow realized her daughter would never change and all hope was gone.

The widow received solace and support from her church family throughout the years. She was very happy, except for these brief times of terror. During one of the church sermons on financial responsibility, the widow thought about her estate assets. She knew in her heart that to leave any money to her daughter would be a serious mistake. In fact, it would probably cause the daughter's death. The thought of leaving any money to Lucy or for her benefit, was totally revolting. Since the widow had adopted this church family as her own, she decided to leave her assets to them.

She made an appointment with a local attorney to draw the Will. She felt very good about her decision to leave her assets to the church. They had always been there for her and had never asked for anything in return. The pastor's wife had nursed her back to health after the terrible beating by her daughter. The attorney gathered the pertinent information.

Then he asked the question, "Where do you want your estate assets to go after your death?"

The widow relayed her sad story about her daughter to the attorney. Then she unhesitatingly said, "I want my church to be the sole beneficiary of my estate. I specifically do not want my daughter to get one dime."

The lawyer advised, "I can draft a Will that leaves your estate to your church, but you must leave your daughter some money. I suggest you leave her at least two thousand dollars. That way, she will only get this money and not be able to say she was omitted by mistake."

The widow was not prepared for this. "Are you telling me I can't leave my estate to whomever I choose?"

"Well," the attorney said, "You must leave your daughter something, and I suggest leaving her two thousand dollars. That will be the only thing she gets. Your estate value is well over $250,000. The church will receive the majority of your estate. This is done so that every one knows you did not leave her out by mistake."

The widow was still very unsatisfied and unhappy. After a time of contemplation the widow agreed. Later, the widow came back to sign the Will. She grumbled when she read the part about leaving two thousand dollars to her daughter. She acknowledged she read and understood the Will. She signed it in the presence of two witnesses and a notary. She left a copy of her Will with the attorney and took the original home with her.

A year later, the widow died of a heart attack unrelated to Lucy's activities. The widow's pastor gathered her personal things, including the Will, and took them to the attorney. After reviewing the Will, the Pastor noticed the attorney's face looked anguished.

The attorney said, "I have some really bad news."

At first the pastor thought there was a problem with the daughter and asked, "Is it the daughter?"

"No, not exactly," the attorney said, "There is a problem with the Will."

"Well how bad could it be?" said the pastor, "You drafted the Will."

"That's right," said the attorney, "but you know she didn't want her daughter to get anything? I had to leave Lucy two thousand dollars to identify her as a child and acknowledge her."

"Okay, so what's the problem?"

The attorney said, "The widow wasn't very happy about leaving Lucy the two thousand dollars. I knew she wasn't happy when she left my office and apparently when she got home she used an exacto knife to cut out the sentence in the Will where Lucy gets the two thousand dollars."

"So what's the problem?"

The lawyer explained, "Under our state law, if the Will is defaced in any way, it is totally invalid. Her use of the exacto knife has defaced the Will."

The pastor was uncomprehending.

The lawyer continued, "That means the widow died without a Will and all her assets will be distributed according to the laws of intestacy. Our state codes provide who gets the estate assets. In this case, when a woman dies without a husband, and without a Will, the only child, Lucy, gets all of her mother's estate. The church gets nothing."

"But that's not what she wanted," protested the pastor.

"I know," said the attorney, "but that's the law. A defaced Will is invalid, even though we can determine the intent."

Legal Analysis: *Most states now have statutory language in place to avoid this tragic result. The statutes and case law allow the Will to stand but the defaced part will be ignored. The daughter will get the two thousand dollars and the church will receive the rest. If the Will is defaced to the point that the Will appears to be destroyed, then the court may declare the intent of the testator was to revoke the Will. If the intent can be determined by looking at the Will, it may be honored. However, any changes such as scratch-outs, pen and ink changes and line-outs will be ignored. Even the exacto knife surgery will be ignored. The legal requirements for the creation of a Will are set up for the protection of the person creating the Will. Without these strict requirements, the opportunity for fraud and trickery is great. After Mom is gone, each kid would say Mom promised them the house and all of the money. If a Will could be changed by just taking a pen and drawing through a small bequest and writing in a larger number, there would be no way to tell if Mom did it herself or the intended beneficiary made the change. This is so even with what appears to be the initials of Mom. Any change in a Will or Trust document must be made with the same formalities as when the original document was signed. This includes signing in the presence of two subscribing witnesses with the proper formalities.*

Deer in the headlights

I heard about this story many years ago. Before you read it, however, you should know there have been changes in the laws in most states that would now alter the outcome.

In this case, a childless married couple was out on the town one evening. They didn't have many worries. The husband's family was very well off and had given the husband much of his wealth. He and his wife were worth in excess of $500,000. Young couples with no children and plenty of money don't do much planning for the future related to death and dying and this couple was no exception. They had no Wills or other estate documents. They left the restaurant after enjoying a nice meal, but husband had a headache and asked his wife to drive. She headed down a small country road and came to an intersection with the main highway. Not familiar with the area, she rolled through the stop sign and into the path of an eighteen-wheel tractor-trailer truck, which was traveling about 55 miles an hour. The truck smashed into the passenger side of the couple's car and both husband and wife were killed instantly. Or were they?

Married with no children and no Wills—who gets their money? If they had a child, that child would inherit all of his parent's assets. The State of Florida, as well as the other 49 states, has laws to see that estates are distributed for the 70% of U.S. citizens who don't have a Will. If you die without a Will ("intestate"), you first look downstream for the beneficiaries. You would look to the children, grandchildren, and great grandchildren, etc. If any exist, then they get the estate. If none, then you look upstream to the parents. If living, they get the assets. If not living, you look for the parent's other children—the deceased couple's brothers and sisters. If there are no living brothers or sisters, you look to their children, the nieces and nephews. If the parents had no children, then you again look upstream to the grandparents. If they are not living, the estate would go to the aunts and uncles of the deceased couple and then to their children and so on.

In our childless couple case, Florida Statutes provide that the surviving spouse gets the estate. Then, upon the surviving spouse's death, the assets go to the surviving spouse's parents. You can now see the dilemma. Which spouse died first? The first one to die would leave everything to the other. At the survivor's death, the assets would go to the survivor's parents. In this case, the parents couldn't agree what to do with the estate. The husband's parents argued that all of the assets of this estate came from their family and therefore should be returned. The wife's family disagreed. The parents sued each other and the case eventually went to trial. The only issue to be decided was who died first. The experts provided conflicting reports. The judge finally ruled that since the husband was in the passenger seat, the seat nearest to the point of impact, he died one moment in time before the wife. Therefore, the wife was the survivor and the wife's parents received all the estate assets.

> ***Legal Analysis:*** *Current Florida Statutes would alter this outcome. If a couple dies at the same time, and there is no evidence to the contrary, then the assets of the estate are split between the parents of each spouse (see F.S. 732.601).*

What it takes to make a Will

Dad is 86 years old has Alzheimer's and other health problems. He had a Will prepared eleven years ago and a codicil two years after that. The terms of the documents provide that all assets are to be distributed to his only heir, the step-daughter he has raised as his own since she was one year old. She has always been the sole heir of the estate. Her Mom died in January and now Dad is lonely and having trouble coping. Since she lives in another state, Daughter asks Dad's sister, who lives nearby, to check on him occasionally. Although Dad and his sister never got along, she agrees. Once inside the house, the sister starts rummaging through the estate documents and is quite surprised when she sees her brother's net worth. He has lived a modest and frugal life and she is shocked to see he has a brokerage statement with a balance in excess of $600,000.

The sister promptly takes her brother to her lawyer for a "Will update." The lawyer meets with Dad for about thirty minutes and after a short discussion, a new Will emerges. Not surprisingly, the new Will reduces the step-daughter's share significantly. The sister now gets fifty percent and the step-daughter gets fifty percent. The step-daughter knows nothing about this last minute change.

Six months after the new Will is signed, Dad dies. When she finds out about the death-bed change, the step-daughter wants to contest the Will. Dad's doctor is interviewed and says Dad was incompetent and unable to understand what he was doing when the change was made. Other friends reported he was unable to remember what he was doing minute to minute and was frequently confused. It seems apparent he was incompetent to sign the new Will. However, the lawyer who prepared the new Will, and his staff, spent thirty minutes with him, and said that in their opinion, Dad was competent.

The standard to make a valid Will is quite low. There are generally three elements that must be met to create a valid Will. If the Testator (signer of the Will) knows he has assets and knows the general nature of those assets the first element is met. Next, if the Testator knows who his heirs might be, the second element is met. Finally, the Testator must understand, at least in a general way, that by signing the Will, his assets will be transferred to those who are named in the Will. If this minimal standard is met, a Testator can create a valid Will.

In the State of Florida, even a person declared legally insane by a court of law can make a valid Will as long as he did so during a lucid moment. This means that under the law, a drunk, drug addict, or delusional person can create a valid Will if it was done during a lucid moment. The lucid moment is usually determined by the lawyer and his staff who prepare and witness the Will.

Legal Analysis: *This low legal standard is consistent in all fifty states.*

The bad daughter

The young lady's eyes were red, puffy and teary. She sat down in the client chair across from my desk and blurted out, "I don't understand. How can this happen? Mom had a Will."

"Why don't you start at the beginning," I said, "and tell me what happened."

She took several deep breaths, wiped her eyes and began to talk. "Mom's health has been declining, so a few years ago she moved from Ohio to Jacksonville, Florida. My sister, Judy, lives there. I'm one of five children. Judy is the oldest and although several of us offered to have Mom move in with us, she chose to live in Jacksonville."

"Did your mom bring any assets with her when she moved to Jacksonville?" I asked.

"She had around $500,000 in assets, most of it in cash, money markets, and CD's. When she got to Jacksonville, she bought a house worth about $45,000."

"Was that titled in her name only?"

She nodded "Yes, I think the deed has her name on it."

I made a few notes. "What about the rest of the assets? How were the bank accounts titled?"

Her lips tightened. "My sister took Mom to several banks and at least one brokerage firm. I know Mom wanted to mainly use banks because of the FDIC insurance. Judy said the bank officers and the stockbroker all suggested that Judy be added to the accounts so that she could help Mom with the accounts. Mom was having problems writing her name because of the arthritis in her hands. It was especially bad in her right hand. That's the one she uses to sign checks. Anyway, Judy said the bank told them that if Mom wanted Judy to write checks, Judy should be on the account too."

She started to cry again. "Mom died last November."

I sat back in my chair. “Let me see if I can finish the story. Your mom died and your sister got all of the assets. Now she doesn’t want to share with the rest of you.”

She looked stunned. “How did you know?”

I smiled slightly. “Lucky guess. Go on.”

Mom’s Will said all her assets must be divided into five equal shares. How can my sister keep all of it?”

“You each have a one-fifth interest in that $45,000 house,” I said, “but the rest of the assets legally belong to your sister and she doesn’t have to divide them with the rest of you. All joint accounts go to the surviving joint account owner. The Will only controls the assets that go through probate. None of the other assets went through probate so, by law, they all belong to the surviving joint account holder, which, as you already know, is your sister.”

“Do you know my brothers won’t even talk to my sister now? This is the worst thing to happen to our family.” She started to cry once more. “I don’t think we will ever be close again.”

“Do you know if your sister plans to share any of the money with the rest of you?”

“She may give us some, but I think she wants to control it.” She looked at me imploringly. “Is there any way to make her follow Mom’s Will? We really need that money.”

I shrugged. “You can sue her.”

She recoiled. “Oh, my god, I’m not going to sue my own sister.”

“Then,” I said, “Other than begging for money, you have no way to force her to do the right thing.”

Legal Analysis: *This is a true example of the “bad daughter” situation. I’m sure very few clients think they have the bad daughter (or bad son) in their family. They believe they have only the good children.*

If the facts were the same as above, but the bad daughter had been a good daughter, what might have happened? After her mom's death she would have all $500,000 in her name only She could prepare 4 checks in the amount of $100,000 each, plus one for herself. One check would be given to each brother and sister. Unfortunately, there is a problem because the good daughter doesn't consider how much she can gift to another sibling without gift tax consequences. The amount she can give to another person without filing a 709 gift tax return is $11,000 (The old amount was $10,000). Any gift greater than $11,000 requires the filing of a 709 gift tax return as well as payment of gift taxes or, more likely, a reduction of the Unified Credit. Each person has a lifetime Unified Credit amount of $1,500,000 (The Unified Death credit is scheduled to increase to $2,000,000 in 2006, but is subject to change at any time by Congress). So even with a good daughter there is an unforeseen gift tax consequence.

Other problems can also surface. Imagine the good daughter has the four checks made payable to each brother and sister. As she is preparing to sign the checks she suffers a massive heart attack and dies on the spot without signing. Now what happens? If she is married, the $400,000 probably goes to her husband. Will he give the money to his sister-in-law and brothers-in-law? Maybe he will, but he certainly doesn't have to. If the sister is divorced or widowed when she dies, the money would go to her children. Are these children (who may not be of legal age for many years) going to transfer the money to their aunts and uncles? It is very clear that once another person is added to your accounts (joint ownership is presumed in most states) you have lost total control of your assets after death. The Will cannot divide the assets the way you desire unless you are the only owner on the account and the account goes through probate.

Do you love me, my money, or both?

Too much money can be a bad thing. Many have said, "I would rather be miserable and rich than miserable and poor!" Unless you've had a lot of money (say twenty million or more), it's hard to imagine the problems. Those of us with children like to think our child's love is simple and unconditional, but if you have a lot of money, sometimes you wonder if it's you or your money that your child loves.

Recently, I met with a very wealthy client to discuss his children and his estate. "I want to avoid inheritance taxes and make sure my estate passes to my children," he said.

I nodded. "That's why I'm here, to help you leave less to the IRS and more to your children."

"Great," he said, "I want to make sure my children get my estate, but I do have a concern. I don't want them to get too much money, because I'm afraid it will spoil them. Actually, I've already spoiled them with too much money, but if I cut off the gravy train, I may lose my family." Seeing the expression on my face he added hastily, "Don't misunderstand me. I love my children, and they're good children, but with all this money coming to them, I foresee nothing but problems. I really need your help, especially since my health is declining."

We discussed several estate planning options and finally I summed up, "I can reduce your estate taxes but the real problem is what your children are going to do with your money once they get it."

He nodded. "That's the problem. I've been cursed with this money and I'm afraid it's going to ruin my children. They are already hitting me up for a sizable advancement."

"How much?" I asked.

"A million dollars each," he said.

I laughed. “Wow, why start at the bottom when you can start at the top?”

He smiled. “That’s not the worst of it. They want the money now, but I’m not sure I want to give it to them. I’ve already given them $600,000 each.”

I said, “Why don’t you just say no?’”

He shook his head. “I’ve tried that already. My daughter didn’t talk to me for almost two years. No, that’s not an option. With my health failing, all I have now is my family.”

“That’s quite a burden on you.”

“Yes, it is, which is why I’m here. Can you give me some options?”

“There are a number of estate planning tools available to accomplish your goal,” I said, “but they all have their costs. Some cost a lot of money, some are expensive to maintain, some relinquish too much control, and others are cumbersome to maintain on a yearly basis. What is more important to you, keeping control of the money or reducing taxes?”

“Both,” he said.

“Then I suggest you give them the money in such a way that it belongs to them, but you still maintain control to ensure it is used properly. You can set up a Corporation, Limited Liability Company, or a Family Limited Partnership, and it will act like a family bank. You loan the money to the children from this bank, but only after they have presented a business plan. Each plan is reviewed by a loan officer, a lawyer, and a CPA. If this loan committee approves the loan, the chances for a successful venture are increased. If the loan committee does not approve the loan, they have to submit another business plan. Although this committee costs money, it increases the odds of your children’s success with their investments. Your children will be pleased because they get the money now to invest and make their fortunes. You’ll be happy because you control the money and know they are making successful investments. Further, additional benefits could be achieved by this planning. First, you could make the loan at a low interest rate and then forgive the repayment, up to $22,000 a year. The lowest interest payment allowed by the IRS today is about 3%. Secondly, the promissory notes could be self-canceling at your death, thereby forgiving any outstanding balance, free of estate taxes.

"Wow, that's more than a mouth-full. In essence, you're saying I don't give them the money outright, but loan it to them. But before the loan is made, each business venture is thoroughly reviewed to measure its likelihood of success?"

"That's it exactly. In a way, you will educate them with their own money while moving money out of your estate, but not spoiling them. They must do their homework and come up with a good business plan, which will increase the chance for their success. You exercise control of the money because you control the loan process."

Legal Analysis: *The preferred legal entity now is a Limited Liability Company or LLC. This entity enjoys all of the benefits of a subchapter S corporation (such as limited liability) but has additional benefits.*

So sue me

This story concerns a very nice gentleman and loving father. One Saturday afternoon, one of his daughters dropped by the house. She desperately wanted a new car, but because of her poor credit rating, she couldn't qualify for the car loan.

She arrived on Dad's doorstep, with the car, and pleaded, "Dad, I want to buy this car, but they say I can't qualify for the loan." Dad looked at the car and at his daughter's big, sad, doe eyes and agreed to help. They drove to the car lot and met with the finance manager. Dad and he discussed the options, and eventually struck a deal requiring Dad to put up some of his CDs for collateral. The CDs could stay at the bank earning interest, but if the daughter failed to make a payment, the finance company would take the CDs to satisfy the outstanding loan balance. The daughter promised she would never miss a payment and she never did.

The real story concerns the way the car was titled and an accident that happened two years later. Because the car was financed with Dad's collateral, the dealership had the title issued jointly in both the daughter and her dad's name. The title read, "Jane Doe or John Smith," but Dad didn't know he was on the title as a joint owner. The daughter didn't understand what this meant and never discussed it with him. She drove the car and made prompt payments on the car loan. Without many assets of her own to protect, she had the car insured for minimum liability amounts as required by state law, currently $10,000 in Florida. Two years after purchasing the car, the daughter was involved in a rear end car accident and was found at fault. The other driver suffered a serious neck injury, hired an attorney and demanded the daughter's insurance company pay their $10,000 policy limits. Like most insurance companies, they refused. The negotiations and discussions continued for several years as the injured person's neck got worse. He eventually underwent a laminectomy (removal of disc material from the spine) as a result of the accident. He lost months of work, pay, benefits, and was living in painful misery. When the negotiations between the insurance company and the injured person's lawyer were not productive, the injured person sued the driver and owners of the at-fault vehicle—both the daughter and her dad.

One fine afternoon, as Dad is sipping ice tea on his front porch, a sheriff's deputy arrives with a summons and complaint naming Dad as a defendant in the lawsuit. He looks at the complaint with unbelieving eyes, wondering how he can be sued when he doesn't even own the car. That's when he learns about the joint title and that he is a co-owner. (I think he had a good argument to be removed from the complaint on the basis that this was an error in title and that he did not know he was on the title. But for reasons unknown to me, he was unable to remove himself from the complaint as a defendant.)

The daughter's car insurance company defended the action. Dad did not have any insurance coverage for this car. His insurance coverage covered only the named cars on his policy. The daughter's car was not on his policy and therefore he had no insurance protection. After several years in litigation, the case finally went to trial. It ended after two days with a judgment against daughter and dad for $287,000. After another year of legal maneuvers and an appeal, the judgment swelled to almost $600,000. Eventually, the daughter's insurance company tendered its $10,000 limits, which was all that was required of them. The daughter had no money so Dad was left owing the $590,000 balance.

The Dad didn't contact me until after the judgment was entered. Although I was able to make a few suggestions, asset protection planning is generally futile after the Sheriff knocks on your door. In this case, because the insurance company could have settled the case early for $10,000, but refused, they acted in "bad faith." The plaintiff's lawyer was very diligent and eventually forced the bad faith insurance company to pay the entire judgment, freeing my client from this debt.

Legal Analysis: *Under the dangerous instrumentality doctrine in Florida, all joint owners of a car are liable for any injuries and/or damages caused by the car, unless it has been stolen. Imagine that your son is off at college and he loans his car, which is also titled in your name, to a friend. This friend is involved in a car accident which severely injures someone. You are liable as a joint owner. My advice to all parents with children 18 years or older is to title the car in the child's name. You can still include the car on your insurance policy, but you will be relieved of this extra liability.*

I've got one of those

One afternoon in my office I was discussing the problems related to Alzheimer's with a nice elderly couple. They listened intently and the wife asked several questions. I started talking about the particular problems one faces with an Alzheimer's patient and said, "As the disease progresses, the short term memory suffers. Many people with Alzheimer's don't think they have anything wrong with their memory and if challenged they sometimes become belligerent." As I said this, the wife put her hand up in front of her to block her husband's view. She winked at me and indicated with the roll of her eyes that her husband was just such a person. He never noticed.

An individual who turns age 65 has a 43% chance of spending some time in a nursing home.

They took my child and there is nothing I can do

It was a typical Sunday afternoon, crisp, warm, and sunny. Dot and Buck were relaxing after a very filling Sunday supper. They attended church in the morning and heard the sermon on giving and reaching out. The preacher said you should share your faith and love with others. Dot and Buck were talking about that very subject, trying to decide how it applied to them. As they discussed this, a car drove up in the driveway. It was Dot's niece Lucy and her current boyfriend, Bart. Lucy and Bart had a one-year-old daughter, Cheyenne. Cheyenne was the sweetest, cutest little baby girl Dot had ever seen. Dot held this precious little bundle of joy the entire time Lucy and Bart were visiting.

After several hours, Lucy finally got the nerve to make her announcement. "Aunt Dot, Bart and I are going through a rough time. We are not really making ends meet and we need to move around a lot. We are not able to take Cheyenne with us and were wondering if you and Uncle Buck could take care of Cheyenne for a while?"

Dot and Buck were shocked. A newborn child in the house after all these years was not something they were prepared for. Both of their daughters were in their mid-twenties, and there were no grandchildren.

Buck was totally silent. Dot stammered a bit when she said, "We can watch her for a couple of days but not longer than that. We can't do this on a full-time basis. We just can't do it. We have our life set in certain ways and there is no way we can have a baby here for a long period of time."

It appeared Lucy was slightly disappointed but she said that would be okay. They would be back in a couple of days and pick up Cheyenne.

As the days passed, Cheyenne chipped away at the hearts of Uncle Buck and Aunt Dot. They were not really disappointed when Lucy didn't show three days later as she promised. They felt the tug of that maternal instinct. The sharing of their faith and love with Cheyenne must have been what the preacher was talking about. They were convinced Cheyenne was destined to be reared by them.

After several weeks with no word from Lucy, the call finally came. Lucy was high on something. She asked how Cheyenne was doing. She did not offer an explanation about her absence or an apology. She made an off-hand comment about coming to get her daughter, but it passed. It was that moment Dot realized she loved Cheyenne and letting her go back to her mother and wander about the countryside was not an option. Unfortunately, Dot was not the mother and she had no legal rights. She and Buck decided to do nothing and just hope Lucy did not want to come and get her daughter.

After six months Lucy came for a visit. Dot's blood pressure was at an all-time high. Buck wasn't much better. Their stomachs were in knots. Finally, with a great sigh of relief, Lucy left, alone. She spent time with Cheyenne and cried about not being able to take care of her. She remarked how well Cheyenne looked and how much she had grown. Lucy said she was trying to get her life together and as soon as she could do that she would return for Cheyenne.

After this six-month visit, Dot and Buck made an appointment to see me. They relayed the series of events leading up to that time. They acknowledged they were in love with Cheyenne and thought of her as their own daughter. The thought of Lucy coming for Cheyenne in the middle of the night, and taking her on the road somewhere, had them terrified. I said, "Unfortunately, Cheyenne is not your child. You have no parental rights. You have no custody rights. You have no rights at all now. Lucy can take her daughter any time she wants. It probably won't be in the middle of the night, but it will be just as bad for you. Your only hope of helping Cheyenne is to get temporary custody so you have some claim. You can't even take her to the doctor now because you don't have any legal authority over her."

Dot sat up a bit when I said that. She offered, "It's really hard for us. At first we thought we would just look after her for several days. But now, after six months, there is no way we can part with her. She would not be safe with her mother."

I said, "I understand your feelings. The problem is that if you didn't let Lucy have her daughter she could have you charged for not releasing her daughter. I'm sure Lucy could clean up well enough to convince a judge she is a proper mother. Your ties to Cheyenne would be severed forever."

Dot started to cry. "I know how I feel now. I can't imagine how I will feel in one or two years. How could I ever let her go, then?"

I said, "You've hit the nail on the head. The point is—how do you protect your heart from being broken by the loss of Cheyenne? Even though you know Lucy is a terrible mother, she is still her mother. You are not. You have no claim or legal rights. It's my advice for you and Buck move forward to get—at a minimum—temporary custody of Cheyenne. Then later, you might be able to get permanent custody of her. If you ever find the right time to take advantage of Lucy, I recommend you do so. It could be money or something else. You are doing it so Cheyenne can have a better life. I am assuming you can provide a better life for Cheyenne?"

Dot answered empathically, "Oh, Yes, Buck and I will devote our lives to her. It's hard to imagine how much our lives have changed in the last six months. Now I can't imagine being without her. We have started a college program for her."

I said, "What would her life be like with Lucy?"

She said, "Lucy has three other children from two different fathers. They are parceled out with Lucy's mother and one sister. There is no way Cheyenne would be better off with her mother, who can't even take care of her other three children."

I said, "You have no protection now. It's dangerous for you and Cheyenne. You need to call Lucy and tell her to come and pick up Cheyenne unless she signs a temporary custody agreement."

Dot was shaking her head looking at me like I had lost my mind, saying, "No, no, we can't do that. We don't want to lose her."

I continued, "You can't live each day not knowing if Lucy will come to the house unexpectedly and then legally and rightfully take Cheyenne from you and Buck. You must have some legal right to keep her. Then, after a period of time, you can move forward and increase your legal rights. Ultimately, you will want Lucy and Cheyenne's father to sign away legal rights allowing you and Buck to adopt her. You can tell Lucy this is for Cheyenne's protection. That is true, but it will also be for your peace of mind. You've got to do something. You just can't live your life this way. I say put it to the test and tell Lucy to come sign the papers or pick up Cheyenne."

Dot was shaking her head in a way suggesting "no way." "I don't know about that. What if Lucy comes and picks her up and takes her somewhere else? I want to wait and see. I now understand my options. I think its best to wait and take the risk."

I said, "Okay. You can wait and see what develops. Maybe, over time, Lucy will see how well off Cheyenne is and leave her with you. However, she may see how attached you are and threaten to take Cheyenne from you unless you give Lucy money. There are many options. What is the right thing to do? I don't know. It's not often I'm stumped. I don't think there is a right answer here. Waiting may be just a good as pressing the issue now. You know I'm for pressing the issue now. If you lose Cheyenne now, although it will be hard on you, it will be easier than having her snatched from you after several years."

Waiting ultimately paid off for Dot and Buck. After several years, Dot requested Lucy and Bart sign over legal custody, which they did. Lucy had given birth to another baby and this was just one less problem to deal with. Dot and Buck are happy and Cheyenne is growing up a loved, healthy, and happy child.

My kids are Peeping Toms

"This is my second marriage of seven years and I want my wife to have full use of my house after I'm gone. I want her to have a place to live with no worries. She doesn't have to pay rent or pay for any major repairs. I feel like I've taken care of her by providing the house. She will also get my military retirement pay once I'm gone. She will have plenty of money and will not have to pay for a place to live," stated the elderly gentleman.

"That's great," I replied, "I reviewed your prenuptial and you certainly don't have to let her live in your house rent free. You could have kicked her out and given the house to your kids. That's very kind of you. I will add this to your Trust as a devise. If she survives you—which she probably will, since she is 20 years younger than you—she can live in your house, rent free, for the rest of her life."

He thought about that for a minute. "You know, I've been thinking about this. If she remarries, I want to terminate her right to live in my house. It can go to my kids right then. I don't think I want to support some young stud staying rent free in my house."

"You want to terminate the life interest your wife has in your house if she gets married?"

"That's right, if she gets remarried, this new guy can pay for a place for her to live, not me."

"I can tell you right now what's going to happen. Your wife will never get remarried. She will just have this young stud move in with her and live rent free in your house."

My client started wiggling in his seat. Clearly, he was getting a little antsy about this. It may have been a subconscious fear. He said, "You're right. If she remarries or has a boyfriend live with her, she will lose the right to live in the house."

"Do you know what you have just done?"

"What are you talking about?"

“You have just turned your children into peeping toms. They will have to follow her around and peep in her windows and see if anyone is living with her. And that’s not the only problem. What if the guy only spends one night or one week? Where is the cut-off. Can you see the problems?”

He settled down a bit with a resigned look in his face. “You’re right. Let her have the house. Whatever happens, happens.”

Legal Analysis: *Some conditions in a Will or Trust are very hard to enforce. Most estate attorneys try to discourage conditions as part of bequests. However, certain conditions—such as reaching a certain age or completing college—are routinely enforced.*

Mom got kicked out of her own house

After one of my workshops, a gentleman approached me and asked a few questions about estate planning. His questions were a little too involved for the time I had left after the workshop, as several other attendees were waiting to ask their own questions. He scheduled a meeting with me the next week to discuss what he described as a "very unusual situation."

At the meeting the next week I asked him, "What's this unusual situation you mentioned?"

He began, "Let me tell you a story. My mother is a very generous soul, but she does have her difficult moments. She has two sons—my brother and me—and several years ago, she decided to do some estate planning. She is very frugal and did not want to spend the money it would take to consult a lawyer. A friend of hers had transferred a house to her son with no problems, so Mom thought she could do the same thing with my brother and me. She eventually deeded the beach house to me and her home in town to my brother."

I asked, "Did she use a quit-claim deed to make the transfer?"

He nodded, yes.

"Did she reserve a life estate in either of these properties?" I could tell from his puzzled expression that he did not understand the term. "Did she retain the right to live in and use these properties for the rest of her life?"

"No, the deeds transferred the property to me and my brother with no strings attached."

I nodded. "What happened next?"

He looked away for a minute and then softly said, "I'm embarrassed to tell you this. One night my brother and his wife were eating dinner with my mother at her house. There was an argument of some kind—I'm not sure what it was about—but it got pretty heated. I think my mother said something about my brother's wife, so my brother got up and ordered my mother out of the house. My mother said, 'This is my house!' But my brother said, 'No it's not! You gave it to me and I want you out!' My brother and his wife left, but several days later, my brother's lawyer contacted my mother and told her she was no longer the owner of the house and would have to leave. Of course she was devastated, but she is also a stubborn and prideful woman and she didn't call me for a while. She packed her bags and was able to rent the house next door to her home.

My brother and his wife moved into my mother's home and they live there now. My mother rents the house next door to them because she liked the neighbors and the neighborhood. By the time I found out about this situation it was already out of control. I tried to talk sense to my brother, but it was too late." He sighed. "I don't think my brother and mother have said two words to each other since that night."

I could only shake my head. "Well, this is a first for me. I never thought a child could be that cold-blooded. What have you done with your property?"

He answered, "I rent it out and give Mom the money. It helps supplement her social security income. Unfortunately, the rent for the beach house is not that much and she is barely scraping by. She is using her cash investments to pay for her rent instead of saving it or spending it on vacations. It's a really sad situation."

I said, "I tell people at my workshops and my clients about the perils of deeding property to their kids and this is one possible result. Most parents say 'that will never happen to me,' and of course most are correct. But situations like this are why I rarely recommend titling property jointly with a child or giving the home to a child while still living in it. And there can be other problems. For instance, suppose your brother didn't pay his taxes or lost a big lawsuit. The IRS could take his half of the house. There are so many unforeseen consequences of giving away an asset like this or titling it jointly with a child. I wrote a book on estate planning and devoted an entire chapter to the problems of giving away assets or titling assets jointly with children."

"You don't have to worry about me," he replied. "I've learned the lesson, but I still can't believe this has happened. My mother, my brother, and I are living proof of estate planning gone wrong."

Legal Analysis: *The problem with giving a joint interest in real property (land) to a child or deeding the entire interest is as follows:*

1. Any transfer of interest greater than $11,000 subjects the giver to the filing of a 706 gift tax return.

2. Any gifts in excess of the gifting limits (consult your CPA or Tax Attorney for the limits affecting you) will require the payment of gift taxes.

3. Jointly owned property with rights of survivorship goes to the joint owner instead of the heirs named in the Will.

4. A debt including an IRS lien, judgment creditor, or Bankruptcy Trustee will compromise the ownership of the property. A creditor can force the sale of the property.

5. When another name is added to the deed, two names are required to sell. A child must be consulted before a sale can occur.

6. The liability of the joint owner spreads to the original owner. In other words, Mom is now liable for the debts of her son.

Easy come, easy go—The plight of lottery winnings and inheritances

Here's something you can take to the bank: If you are age thirty or younger and win the lottery or receive a sizeable inheritance, it will be gone in ten years or less. But the older you are the more likely you are to keep the unearned booty. In my experience, a person over fifty-five has a much better chance of holding onto the money. It is amazing how many lottery winners end-up filing bankruptcy. If you didn't have the discipline to make the money in the first place, it is unlikely you will have the discipline to keep it.

When people over fifty-five receive a substantial windfall, most do not radically alter their standard of living. Most are already retired or nearing retirement and have all they want or need. A seventy-one-year-old client of mine won \$3.5 million dollars in the lottery. He bought a new set of tires for his car, a new dishwasher and he and his wife took a cruise. His lifestyle was already set and the infusion of new money did not change it much. Of course after his death, his children will have a great time with the money, which has been conservatively invested and continues to grow.

If a son in his thirties inherits \$1.5 million dollars, while technically a millionaire, he cannot live a millionaire's lifestyle. A young man will, for example, purchase a fancy new house, two new cars, a good-sized motor home, a boat, some expensive jewelry for his wife and a membership in the exclusive hunting club. Since he lives in a new neighborhood, he will need a new wardrobe, a big screen TV and the home entertainment system. In just a few weeks, over one-third of the inheritance has vanished. If the remaining one million is invested at five percent he would have an annual return of fifty thousand dollars before taxes. This is perhaps thirty-five thousand after taxes, hardly the income necessary to join the jet-set, especially if you just told the boss "take this job and shove it." Meanwhile, the bills keep on coming. Electricity on the new house alone is costing him over \$600 a month. To pay the taxes on the new house and continue the lifestyle, he must pull a hundred-thousand dollars from the principle. It's no big deal, since there is still over nine hundred thousand dollars left in the account. Next year the income is down to forty-five thousand dollars and he makes another hundred-thousand dollar withdrawal.

Now the account is down to eight hundred thousand dollars and shrinking. It's going the wrong way so our new millionaire decides it's time for aggressive action. After many solicitations for investment opportunities he sinks two hundred thousand dollars into a new restaurant chain "guaranteed" to make it big. "Sinks" turns out to be the operative term as the money quickly disappears without a trace. Now the account is down to six hundred thousand dollars—two-thirds, gone in two years with no slowdown in spending. It will be completely gone in ten years.

I had a 22 year-old client who was to receive more than a million dollar personal injury settlement for the death of his wife. I asked him if he would like to receive a lot of money on a regular basis and still be able to retire with millions of dollars. He was interested and asked me to tell him more.

I said "After the settlement is received, take two hundred thousand dollars and keep it in your own account. Spend it, blow it, invest it, it doesn't matter; do whatever you want with it, but keep your job. Place the remaining eight hundred thousand dollars in an irrevocable Trust that is locked for ten years. After a 7.2% return (long-term bonds, for example), the account doubles, and is now worth $1.6 million. At the ten-year mark, take five hundred thousand dollars into your own account and lock up the remaining $1.1 million for an additional ten years. After the next ten year period, the account is now valued at $2.2 million. Now you are forty-two and you can put an additional eight hundred thousand dollars into your own account. Lock the remaining $1.4 million into the Trust. Ten years later, at age fifty-two, the account now holds $2.8 million. Take one million and lock the remaining balance in the Trust account for the next ten years. At age sixty-two, when many are thinking about retirement, you will unlock $3.6 million from this Trust. You have had the opportunity to spend and enjoy the money throughout your life and yet there is more than enough to provide you with a comfortable retirement."

My client looked amazed. He said, "That sounds great."

"So," I said, "Do you want to do it?"

He looked at me, smiled and said, "No, I think I can do it on my own."

Sell me some life insurance

Have you ever wondered how much insurance is enough? For a young couple there is a simple rule of thumb. Determine the husband's income, for example, $75,000. The average young couple spends almost all of their yearly income. If the husband suffered an untimely death, the household expenses do not drop by half. Most of the time the expenses continue, but for a few minor items; sweat socks, underwear, fishing lures and jock itch cream. If the husband has $750,000 in Life Insurance and this amount is invested at 10% interest, the yearly return is $75,000 before tax. If the proceeds are invested at CD rates, of around 3%, then the yearly return is $22,500. This is a fraction of what the wife needs to live on without invading the principal. Once the principal is invaded, the financial pot quickly declines leaving little for the long-term needs of the wife and children. The wife may be forced to get a job to help ends meet. This may take her away from the children at a time when they need her most. Also, leaving a wife financially secure minimizes the likelihood of her marrying a new man. This new man would step in as the new father of your children.

Term life insurance is dirt-cheap for most healthy young people. A twenty-year term policy which protects the family during critical years, when children are growing up, is a good option. This should be part of the family budget like buying food and paying a mortgage payment. This couple should consider at least a one million dollar policy. If the husband's benefit is invested at long-term rates of 6% to 7% she would probably survive without needing to invade the principal.

Legal Analysis: *I am not an insurance salesman. However, the math here is quite simple. In my opinion, term insurance covering the critical years when children are in the home and then going to college, is a necessity. Whole life insurance is great for a long term investment. Unfortunately, it provides little financial benefit to a young family in the event of an untimely death.*

Too much trouble for me, but my wife can handle it

The crusty old guy looked as though he had accumulated several lifetimes of experience. Seventy-three years-old, he gave the impression that everything that could happen to him had happened to him, that he had learned from these experiences and been successful because of them. We were meeting in my office and I commented, "I understand you have several car painting businesses located in several different cities."

He said, "Yes, I do. I started from one little paint and body shop here and expanded over the years to six different cities. I now have eight paint and body shops. It keeps me pretty busy, but I've been having some health problems and I can't get around like I used to."

"What are you going to do now that your health is preventing you from managing the stores?"

He responded, "I'm not sure what I'm going to do. None of my children are interested in the business."

"I suggest you sell your businesses now. You should liquidate all of your complicated business holdings," I said.

You would have thought I had just asked him to sell his first-born child. "No way!" he said defiantly. "I'll never sell my businesses. Besides, you don't realize the problems and time it would take to sell these shops."

"I understand it will take a lot of time and effort," I admitted, "but if you sell the business, don't you think you could get a better selling price than if your wife tried to sell it?"

He nodded, "There's no doubt I could get more money than anybody else. I'm the only one who can convey the true value of this business. I built it from the ground up. No one helped me."

I waited for a minute and then said, "If you sold the business, don't you think you could save on the expenses of a sale? If you were gone, your wife would have to hire a lawyer and pay for his sales help."

"Are you kidding?" he said, "Most lawyers are blood-sucking fee machines—present company excluded, of course. There is no doubt I could sell the business myself and save a lot of money. My lawyer could just draw up the sales agreement and any security agreement needed, unless it was a cash deal."

I let his statement hang in the air for a moment and then he said, "So you're trying to tell me I can get a higher sales price and save on the selling expenses if I do it myself, rather than let my wife do it after I'm gone."

"I couldn't have said it better myself," I agreed. "Why not leave your wife cash and security instead of burdening her with the job of running a business or selling it when she can no longer run it?"

He said he would think about it before he made any other plans and then he left. I never heard from him again. I doubt if he ever made any plans, which means his wife and children will have to clean up his mess after he's gone and try to sell the business for what they can get.

Legal Analysis: *A major goal of estate planning is to streamline the estate. Effort should be made to reduce the complexity of the estate and consolidate assets. It is much easier to transfer a three-million dollar brokerage account than sell six paint and body shops and then make distributions.*

The worst day of my life

There are few times in your life when you feel a pain that rocks your soul. Losing a child, a spouse, or a parent certainly fall in this category. But other events can cause almost as much pain, as a client of mine recently discovered. His elderly father was living at home. He had been very independent and had not required much assistance, but it was clear that he was beginning to slip a little. One evening, Dad was heating his dinner and left the pan on the stove while he went into the family room to watch TV for a minute. The pan caught on fire and smoke billowed out of the kitchen into the rest of the house. Luckily, a neighbor saw the smoke, called 911, and the firefighters arrived in time to douse the fire. Although the kitchen suffered major smoke damage, the rest of the house was fine after a good airing out. No one was injured. Dad was a little scared, but he was all right.

Now the son (my client) was faced with the decision of what to do. The Department of Children and Families did an investigation and the son was told his dad could no longer be left at home, because he was a danger to himself and others. Dad's mental condition continued to decline and he was starting to be a real problem. The son's wife worked and his children were very young. Space was limited at the son's house and it was clear that Dad would require more care than his son could offer. There were no other family options, so the son talked to Dad about a nursing home, but Dad was adamant. He would never agree to go to a nursing home. The son finally had to make a decision none of us would ever want to make. He would be forced to have Dad declared incompetent and placed in a nursing home against his will. Before this legal procedure was initiated, the son asked his dad if he wanted to go for a car ride. Dad agreed and they went to the grocery store. Then the son stopped at the back entrance of a nursing home. He walked with Dad through the building. It was clear his dad didn't know where they were. When they got to the front entrance, the son stepped through the gate and closed it behind him.

Dad was puzzled. Then his son told him, "Dad, you've got to stay here. It's for your own good."

My client had tears in his eyes as he said, "As I started to leave, my dad gripped the chain link fence, shaking it and pleading, 'Don't leave me here. Don't leave me here.' I think that image will be burned in my mind for the rest of my life."

Legal Analysis: *An adult child who takes care of a parent assumes certain responsibilities. The home must be safe and clean. If a parent has medical problems then the parent should be taken to the doctor. If a child is unable or unwilling to do these things, the child should notify the Department of Children and Families and inform them of the situation. A home study will be done and certain actions can be taken. The benefit to the child is that the child is no longer responsible. The Department can recommend a guardianship and someone other than the child will act as the guardian. If a parent is left neglected by this child that child could face criminal charges. If the Department takes over, the child will most likely never have any control over their parent again, but of course the child will no longer have the responsibility either.*

Bing Crosby's 62 year old brat

There are a few famous people who have interesting estates. Bing Crosby is one whose estate problems are legendary among Estate Trust lawyers. When Bing's first wife Dixie died, the Will and Inventory were made public because filing the Will and Inventory in the probate clerk's office makes them a public record. Anyone willing to spend $1 per page can ask for and receive a copy of the estate documents. Needless to say, the tabloids were interested in Bing Crosby's estate after his wife's death. They obtained and published copies of his wife's Will with its instructions. Bing's Will was a mirror of his wife's Will so every one knew his instructions. The Inventory is also a public record available for public review. The Inventory showed how much money, assets, and debt he had. This all was very difficult and embarrassing for Bing, who was quite a private person. He was questioned about his most private and personal matters, such as why he put certain people in and left others out and the public got to read about all of it. Questions were asked about the way he raised his children and how they turned out.

Bing learned from this mistake and when he died in the early 70s there was no mention of his Will, estate, assets, instructions or any reference to his children. He had established a Living Revocable Trust that kept all of his family and financial matters private. One interesting item, however, escaped this veil of secrecy, and it has traveled in estate lawyer circles for years.

Crosby's oldest son, Gary, was not the most trustworthy of characters. Bing recognized this and directed his trustee to hold the Trust assets for Gary until he was sufficiently mature to handle the money. In Bing's opinion, this was at age sixty-five. Unfortunately, Gary died in 1995, before reaching his sixty-fifth birthday. I don't know where the assets went. Perhaps they went to Gary's children or they may be held in the Trust estate and directed to someone else.

Legal Analysis: *A Living Revocable Trust is a Will substitute. A Will is your last letter of instruction. It says where things go after you are gone. A Trust, like a Will, also says where things go* *after you are gone, but a Will requires probate and a Trust does not. A Will is a public document because it is recorded in the Probate clerks' office. It, as well as all other probate documents, can be examined for free. Copies usually cost between fifty cents and one dollar per page.*

A Trust allows control of your money after your death. You can also control the timing of your distributions, and the amounts. Some clients want the entire estate distributed to their children immediately after their deaths. Others want to make sure their children are mature enough to handle the money.

In the case of Bing Crosby, he wanted to make sure his son, Gary, would handle the money in a responsible way. Apparently, Gary had been into drugs and alcohol and probably would have squandered the money if he got it at an early age.

How to cut yourself out of the Will

A very lovely lady in her late 60s was in my office. She was there to complete her estate planning after recently moving from another state. Before we started discussing her assets, she slid certain documents across my desk to me, including a letter, and said, "Before we get started, you should know a little about my situation. My husband died five years ago. He left me an estate worth around one million dollars. Not long after his death, my son started a legal action to have me declared incompetent. I presume he did this to gain control of the assets my husband left me."

I queried, "Was this son from your husband's prior marriage?"

"No," she responded, "I understand why you might think that. No, this is my son and he wanted control of my assets. I think you need to review the letter from my attorney who represented me."

I read the letter. The attorney started his letter by saying, "To any lawyer reading this letter and preparing estate documents for this client, please be aware of the following." He went on to detail the events of the husband's death, the probate, the son's quest for control and the incompetency proceeding declaring my client, competent. The attorney warned any estate planning lawyer helping this woman to be armed with foreknowledge that a Will or Trust contest by this son is sure to follow her death.

"Wow, what a story," I said, shaking my head.

"I know. I'm very embarrassed about it," she said quietly, wiping a tear from her cheek. "As you can see, I have a very unusual situation. I would like to leave all of my estate assets to my other son and none to this son. I don't want him to get any of my estate. I spent a lot of money defending the probate and incompetency hearing, and that's all he's going to get."

I assured her, "I understand the situation. I can take certain precautions if I have foreknowledge that a Will or Trust contest is likely to occur. Most of the time I don't know about a contest action until after the client has died. Then it is too late to do this special planning."

“Whatever it takes, I want my estate set-up so he can’t contest it.”

“I can’t guarantee he won’t contest the Trust because anyone can contest an estate document. However, with this planning, the likelihood of a successful Trust contest, one where he sets the Trust aside and gets a share from the court, will be dramatically reduced.” A lawyer can’t make a guarantee because it is unethical to do so. However, most lawyers will say something like, it’s “fairly unbreakable” or it is “unlikely to have problems.”

“That’s what I want. I have about three million in real property and stock investments.”

“So you’ve increased your estate by two million in the last five years?”

She laughed, “No one knew I was such a financial whiz.”

“All right, your estate is about three million. We will discuss the estate tax issue later. You want to leave all of your assets to your one son and leave nothing to your other son. And you want to take every precaution that your wayward son will not be successful with the Will and Trust contest action we know he will file after your death.”

“That sums it up in nutshell.”

I explained to her the general rule of law regarding a Will or Trust contest. A Will or Trust contest is brought generally on two grounds. One is competency and the other is undue influence. The first issue concerns your mental state when you signed the Will. Did you possess the mental capacity to understand what you were doing at the time the Will or Trust was signed? The second issue concerns whether or not you were unduly influenced to the point that you are not exercising your own free will. Both of these grounds involve the mental capacity of the person creating the Will or Trust. A lawyer and his staff are usually the only ones to judge the mental capacity of the person signing the Will and Trust. Their acknowledgement and signing of the document is generally sufficient evidence of capacity and lack of undue influence. However, if a lawyer knows of a potential problem then certain precautions can be taken.

I suggested to her, “Since we know your son will file a legal contest action to set aside the Will and Trust, we should take additional precautions. You will need to meet with a psychologist for a mental evaluation. He will examine you with his own evaluation forms and he will complete an additional evaluation for legal capacity using evaluation forms I supply."

She agreed, "I'll do what ever it takes."

"Okay, I'll arrange the exam for you. When the examination is complete, the Doctor will prepare a written report. I presume you will pass with no problems. I will then schedule a time to execute your Trust. A video photographer will attend the signing conference to video tape the proceedings." She agreed to go forward with my suggestions. I arranged for the psychologist to evaluate her. He gave her a battery of tests to check on her grip with reality and her capacity. I forwarded four pages of legal questions for the Doctor to ask her related to the legal test for capacity under Florida law. The psychologist evaluated her and determined that, in his opinion, she possessed the necessary mental capacity to understand what she was doing. She passed all of the tests with a near perfect score. She articulated her problem with her son and set forth very logical and understandable reasons for wanting to omit this son as a beneficiary from her estate. After receiving notice that her tests were complete, I scheduled the signing conference with the video photographer.

At the signing conference, the video camera recorded the proceedings. I reviewed each legal document with my client. I asked her about her estate assets. She was able to account for her assets in great detail. I asked if she knew what would happen when she signed the Will and Trust documents. She said she believed the assets of her estate would be controlled by these documents and would be distributed according to her directions in the Will and Trust. I next asked her to discuss her family members. She said she had two boys. Then she looked directly into the camera and said, "I know I have two sons but I want to make sure that my son [Johnny] does not receive any of my assets after my death." The signing conference was concluded with her taking her executed Will and Trust documents home in the three-ring portfolio I prepare for my clients.

At her death, when the Will and Trust contest is pursued by her son, I want to be involved. I want to present the psychologist's report along with the videotape. I want to see the look on the judge's face when my client looks at him through the camera lens and says "I know I have two sons but I want to make sure that my son [Johnny] does not receive any of my assets after my death."

I am not aware of any better way to create an estate plan that will survive a Will and Trust contest. This estate plan is as bullet proof as I can make it. It became my model for other estates I felt were potential contest cases. When I do not want to be the primary decision maker about capacity, I send my client to a psychologist or psychiatrist for a mental evaluation. This evaluation added very little to the expense of the estate plan (about $300.00) but I am sure it will save thousands of dollars after her death. As an attorney representing a Will or Trust contestant, I would be very reluctant to proceed if I learned the decedent video-taped the signing conference and had just completed a positive psychological evaluation. Many Will and Trust contestants may no longer pursue a legal action if they learn of the extraordinary measures taken.

As an epilog to this story, I received a call from my client six years after the Will and Trust documents were completed.

She said, "Mark, you're not going to believe what has happened."

I replied, "Don't tell me."

She laughed, "It's true, my son and I have reconciled. I want to change my estate plan so that now he gets a small share!"

Legal Analysis: *Most estates do not need the extraordinary measures taken above. Sometimes I see a client who I feel is on the borderline of mental capacity. If this client wants to change the estate plan from a Will to a Living Trust, with the same beneficiaries, I will usually help. In this case, the client is not making any estate changes, just trying to avoid probate. However, if the client wants to omit a child or make some other drastic change in their estate plan, I recommend the client seek a psychological evaluation. I do not want to bear the sole burden of attesting to mental capacity.*

I feel a client can do whatever they want with their own money. They can give more to one child, leave one child out, or leave it all to charity. My job is to make sure their desire is legally carried out. A criminal defense lawyer loses when his client goes to jail. A personal injury lawyer loses when his client doesn't get any money. An estate lawyer loses when his Will or Trust document is set aside by the court. I take every precaution to ensure my Will and Trust documents will be honored by the court, no matter how vigorously someone tries to contest them.

Generally speaking, a person wanting to create a Will (the "creator") possesses the mental capacity to create a legal Will if the creator can give affirmative answers to a three question test. First, the lawyer asks "Do you know you have assets and can you describe them in a general way?" The creator responds "I have a house, a checking account, and some stocks." An exact accounting is not needed, only a general understanding of the assets. Second, the lawyer asks "Can you tell me about your children and family?" The creator responds "I have two children and some nieces and nephews. But I want my estate to go to my one child who is here taking care of me." A general understanding of the family relations is met with this reply. The last question the lawyer asks is "Do you understand this Will transfers your assets to the child you named in your Will, after your death?" The client responds "Yes, I understand the Will transfers my assets to my son and directs that my other son receive nothing." The third question is answered affirmatively and the creator is presumed to possess the mental capacity to create a valid Will or Trust. This general mental capacity test is similar for most states, but it does vary.

It's outta my estate, or is it?

A very sharp elderly client of mine saw me for an estate review. He said, "I established a brokerage account for my grandson twelve years ago and have been gifting $10,000 each year into his account." He smiled. "I have reduced my estate by twelve $10,000 gifts along with the interest and appreciation on them. The account now has a current balance of $160,000."

"That's a lot of money, I said. "How old is your grandson?"

"He's sixteen," he said.

"Will he be getting the money when he turns 18?"

He shook his head. "No, I don't think so. I kept my name on the account so he can't take it out unless I give my permission."

"Wait a minute," I said with some alarm. "Let me look at that account statement." He passed it over and I scanned the heading where the account holder names are identified. There on the account was my client's name. "Your name is on this account," I said.

"That's right."

I could only shake my head. "Then I'm afraid all of your tax planning has been wasted. The IRS tax code includes any joint accounts with rights of survivorship on your estate asset list. The entire balance is included, not just half. I presume that if you died today your grandson would get the entire account?"

He nodded yes. "Then this account, the full $160,000, will be included in your estate for inheritance tax consideration."

Legal Analysis: *Many clients desire to reduce their estate size by making the $11,000 gifts (formerly $10,000). Why not give the money to your family rather than the IRS. It's wise and prudent to make these gifts for most larger estates. However, there is one* *major rule that must be followed. You must make a completed gift with no strings attached. If you give the gift with strings attached, the gift may not be removed from your estate. If you have a way to control the gift—such as a joint account—or you can take it back, then it is not a completed gift and it's still in your estate for tax consideration.*

The gift made by my client could have been withdrawn because he was still a joint owner. Further, if the grandson died, the account would come to my client via the rights of survivorship and be included in his taxable estate.

Uniform Transfer to Minors Account problems

One of my clients had $260,000 in a Uniform Transfer to Minors Account for his grandson. He was telling me about this account and how it lowered his estate value for inheritance tax purposes. Unfortunately, he did not consider the consequences of giving $260,000 to a 21-year-old boy, recognizing belatedly, that his grandson was very immature. My client asked how he could keep the money and not let the grandson have access to it. At age 21, in Florida, the boy has access to the money. Some parents or custodians simply do not tell a child he has $260,000 in an account, but since the child must sign a tax return every year he knows he has the money. If the child asserts his legal rights, he will get the money and can do with it as he pleases since it legally belongs to him.

Problems with UTMAs:

1. All assets are taxed at the parents tax rate until the child reaches the age of 14. Therefore, there is no tax benefit until the child is 14.

2. The account must be turned over at age 21 (18 in some states) regardless of the child's situation. He could be on drugs, in jail or completely irresponsible. There is no control or discretion left in the hands of the parent or grandparent.

3. If the custodian dies before the minor reaches the age of 21, the account must go through probate before the account can be retitled. This has been a costly surprise for many of my Trust clients.

4. If the custodian dies before the child reaches the age of 21, all assets of the UTMA are included in the custodian's gross estate for inheritance tax consideration.

Under the new 529 plans recently passed by Congress, the money goes into an account, controlled by the owner, to pay for higher education. Income on the assets is tax deferred and the distribution from the account is tax free, as long as it is used to pay for education expenses. The educational uses are very broad. If your grandson turns out to be a brat, you can skip him and pay for the granddaughter's education instead or pay for a niece or other relative. If your own financial situation takes a downturn, you can pay a 10% penalty and get your money back. Talk to your broker for additional information. Congress is making the rules easier to understand and more liberal.

I got my inheritance — and yours too

Some clients are real suckers when it comes to their children and never seem to learn. If a child wants something or gets in trouble, the client will bail him or her out every time. In one case, my client had five children and was in my office for an estate planning consultation. He wanted to avoid probate and guardianship, and make sure his assets would be fairly and equally divided among his children. But he had a problem. One of his sons had a failing real estate business up North. He would call home and plead for $25,000 to $50,000 to get over the "hump." This happened several times and Dad didn't want to see his investment go down the tubes with the failed business so he kept sending more money to keep the son from filing bankruptcy. Over a two-year period he gave his son more than $150,000. In spite of all the cash gifts, the son still ended up filing bankruptcy. He named his father as a creditor in a Chapter 7 liquidation, so Dad got nothing

The problem for the father—apart from being out $150,000—was how to divide his remaining estate assets among his children. After the $150,000 loss, his estate was down to about $300,000. After much discussion, he decided he wanted a Trust to distribute the assets in five equal shares. When I raised my eyebrows at that he said, "I know what you're thinking, but I still have hope my son will pay off this debt to me."

I laughed and said, "Are you serious?"

He sighed, "Not really, I just say that so I won't feel angry towards him." He shook his head. "It's been hard on me. I don't have the financial cushion I had a couple of years ago. My car is ten years old and I haven't taken a vacation in two years because I don't have the money. I'm trying to live off the interest from my investments, but I'm having a hard time making ends meet. I don't want to think badly of him, but he really did put me in this situation."

"In my opinion," I said, "you put yourself there. If a child asks for money, and you can afford to give it, then do so—no strings attached—but never loan a child money. If you are counting on the money and they can't pay it back, even if the circumstances are beyond their control, you are bound to have negative feelings towards your own child."

He still wanted all five children named as beneficiaries, but felt the one son had already gotten more than his share. After more discussion, I drafted a Living Revocable Trust so that his assets avoided probate and guardianship. In the Trust, he specifically made mention of the $150,000 loan to his son. This was listed as an asset to be taken into account by the Trustee after my client's death. If the loan was repaid by the time Dad died, then the estate would be divided in five equal shares. If the loan was not repaid, then this son's share would be reduced by the amount he had already received. This is called an "Advancement." Practically speaking, unless Dad wins the lottery, this son will get nothing at Dad's death. Unfortunately, the rest of the children will see their shares reduced because of this one son. Dad told me his other children were furious about this situation. I doubt the family relationship will survive this problem. It will always be a source of conflict. This son will never regain the close relationship he had with his father or his siblings before he borrowed the money.

Legal Analysis: *Advancements are a routine part of estate planning. If you have given a child a loan or gift you can account for it in your Will or Trust. Simply say that all Advancements shall be taken into consideration. I generally want my client to mention the advancement in detail such as "the $25,000 gift given to Howard." I also prepare a separate schedule to which a client can refer. This schedule might be titled "Advancements," and would record each gift, each loan and any repayments. Most states assume that any gift made prior to death is just that, a gift. They are not Advancements taken into account after death. You must specifically make mention of the gifts if they are to become an Advancement.*

Why didn't I think of this before?

Most busy people don't think about estate planning—other than a simple Will— until one of two events occurs. The first is retirement; the second the death of a family member or close friend.

Many people decide they are too busy to think about estate planning or think estate planning is just for old people. But once they retire, getting the estate in order becomes a priority, so many of my clients see me within six months of retirement. The death of a family member or close friend also brings estate planning to the forefront of their minds. Usually it's the mess left after an untimely death. Often they see that nothing was done, the important papers couldn't be located and no one knew how to get the money. They see family fights over money and personal items. It's not what everyone thought would happen. "They just didn't do any planning," is a frequently heard comment and they vow not to let the same situation happen to their family.

My busiest time for estate planning is January and February. More of my clients complete Wills and Trusts during these two months than any other month of the year. I have discovered that the holidays, Thanksgiving through Christmas, put people in a spirit of giving and wanting to get things in order as they spend time with family and loved ones. With the arrival of the New Year, it's time to make a New Year's resolution. "I'm going to do a new Will and get my estate planning done this year. It's first on my list," they say. I schedule my estate planning workshops for the first few weeks in January to make it easier for those who have made this New Year's resolution to get their estate work completed.

Who takes care of Mom?

The lady was led into my office by my secretary. My secretary gave me that look indicating this lady had some serious problems. I sat up attentively.

"How can I help you?" I offered.

She started sobbing and said, "My mom, it's my mom."

"Tell me about your mom. What's the problem?"

She choked out, "I can't take care of her any longer and the hospital is calling my house. They've called five times. They want me to come and get my mother." She barely finished the sentence before continuing to sob for a couple of minutes. She appeared to be at the point of a breakdown.

"Tell me about your mother. Why does the hospital want you to get her?"

"Because she is okay now and they want me to pick her up. They keep calling. I can't get her. I can't bring her back to my house. I haven't been able to sleep. I'm about to lose my job. I've got to support my children. My mother can't be left alone. I can't stay with her and she can't be left alone. My kids come home from school and my mother is there. She can't be left with my children at home alone. I don't know what to do. I can't deal with this anymore. I've tried to get mother into a nursing home but I don't have the money and I can't find any openings." She started to shudder and sob. "You have to help me."

I offered, "If you can't take care of her, then don't pick her up. She will be taken care of. They won't turn her out on the street. Someone will take care of her. If you do nothing, the hospital will probably have a legal guardian appointed to take care of her."

For the first time there was a ray of hope in her grief-stricken eyes. I continued, "If you can't do it, then don't. No one is forcing you to get her. I promise you, life will go on. You take care of your children and your job. Your mother will be taken care of. She looked at me with that face that says "I'm not sure I believe you, but I'm going to take your advice anyway."

She left full of doubt but with no other alternatives. She had to let go for the sake of her own sanity and the welfare of her children. I spoke to the hospital administration and relayed the situation. While they were not happy having to take care of this problem, they did it anyway. A private guardian was called to initiate a guardianship. They were appointed as guardians for the mother and her property. They located a nursing home and placed her on Medicaid. My client now visits her mother regularly in the nursing home, and has a new outlook on life.

> ***Legal Analysis:*** *The Department of Children and Families (formerly HRS) has certain rules regarding senior citizen neglect. If this mother had been left in her home unattended then there could have been legal liability for the daughter. The hospital had control of the mother and had responsibility for her. They could not turn her out on the street. The hospital was left with the problem of making arrangements for the mother's care. They did make the arrangements, and everything worked out well.*

Don't pull the plug!!

"Keep Mom alive. She can still live. I know she doesn't want to die," pleaded the daughter.

"You know she wouldn't want to be kept alive this way," agonized her brother in response.

"But she's still living, she's breathing. The blood is flowing through her veins. We can't do this," cried the daughter.

The son, awash in anguish, grief, and guilt said, "Mom is gone. Our mother is gone. Her body is here, but it's only a shell. Her mind, her spirit, and her soul are gone. I know in my heart she wouldn't want to be lingering here this way."

With angry tears the daughter said, "I won't do it. I won't be a part of this. What you're doing is nothing but murder!"

"How can you say that," he said. "Mom is dead. Her brain ceased functioning last week. She's brain dead, Sister. There's no hope of her ever getting better. She will just lie here with no dignity, being kept alive with all these machines, and rot. If there were even the smallest chance, I would agree with you. But you can see the brain activity." He pointed to a nearby monitor. "There is none. It's a flat line. We should honor Mom's wishes."

"What are you talking about?" his sister said. "What wishes? Mom never talked to me about anything like this."

"I'm sure she didn't," he said. "I imagine she thought you would not agree with her decision. Mom signed a Living Will." He held up an envelope. "Here it is. It states that her last wish is that she be allowed to die with dignity." He turned a page. "It says if she is no longer able to make decisions, and has a terminal illness, and the doctor has determined there is no hope of recovery, she doesn't want to be kept alive on a machine. She wants the plug pulled. Here, read it yourself."

His sister took the document and read very slowly. Then she read it again. She looked at her mother's signature. Two people attesting to her sound mind had witnessed it. "How could Mom sign this?" asked the daughter through her tears.

He sighed. “It’s not my place to pass judgment on what Mom did or did not do, but it’s clear on this point. She didn’t want to be kept alive on a machine. She took the time to hire a lawyer and sign this directive. She is clearly saying she wants the plug pulled. I’m not making the decision. Mom has already made it for herself. I am just here to abide by her wish and see that her directive is carried out.” He looked at her. “Are you going to stand in the way?”

“I don’t know what to do,” she wept.

“Mom is telling us right here what she wants done. I’m giving this Living Will to the doctor and if he moves forward with pulling the plug are you going to stand in the way?”

Sobbing and crying, the daughter said, “No, but I want to be here holding her hand. I can do that, can’t I?”

He embraced her. “Yes, we will both be here and say goodbye together.”

Legal Analysis: *The Living Will probably should be called the “Last Statement of Death” or “Declaration of Death,” because it says, “If I’m being kept alive on a machine and I am not going to make it, pull the plug.” Living Wills became popular after the Karen Ann Quinlin case in 1975. There are many varieties of the Living Will, but most have similar directions. Some are four or five pages long, listing all sorts of medical conditions under which the plug should be pulled. Some limit food and water and direct that no feeding tubes be inserted. Some Living Wills are just one page with the general direction that the plug be pulled when there is no hope of recovery, as determined by the doctor. The Living Will is the final opportunity a person has to leave a written instruction about what should be done. That person is making the final decisions and not the family members.*

A high-octane Living Will in Florida is called a “Do Not Resuscitate Order,” or DNRO. It says “If you see me for any reason, do not give me CPR, do not code me, do not revive or resuscitate me for any reason.” This document should only be used when there is a terminal condition, such as emphysema or cancer.

Surf's up

One very successful client of mine started an investment account for his only child the week he was born. By the time the child graduated from college the account was worth in excess of $700,000. The son was always a well-behaved child growing up. He made good grades in school, he didn't run with a bad crowd, he didn't smoke or drink to excess and was always well mannered and polite. He had ambition, went to college, and got a degree in finance in four years.

The son then went to work for an investment firm in New York City working with other successful young men. Unfortunately, he started running with a fast (and rich) young crowd. This is where his $700,000 stock portfolio became relevant because he could afford to jet-set with his friends. His "friends" introduced him to cocaine, which quickly took a toll on his body and his job performance. It didn't take long for him to lose interest in anything but cocaine. Ultimately, he lost his job and his friends, but he was not without determination. Recognizing he had a serious problem, he managed to wean himself from his coke habit before all his money went up his nose. After he was clean, the boy moved to California to surf.

My client said his son was doing great now, had invested well and had built his portfolio to over a million dollars. I asked him what his son was doing with his life. Dad said he really wasn't doing anything, just surfing and playing and having a good time. Since he had plenty of money, he didn't have to work.

While he had an easy life it was obvious to me he also had no real direction, no real purpose, no goals. "Does he have any direction?" I asked.

Dad shook his head, "No, he really isn't doing anything meaningful right now." After reflecting a minute, Dad looked at me and said, "If I could do it over again, I wouldn't have established that account for my son. I think it ruined him. The money took away his incentive to learn from his mistakes and grow into a responsible adult. I'm hoping for the best, but I think I made a mistake."

To grow into a mature adult you need drive, goals and ambition. Developing a strong work ethic, overcoming obstacles, and learning from mistakes and setbacks are all part of the process. This Dad belatedly recognized that although he had good intentions, he had deprived his son of these valuable learned experiences.

Which child gets the family vacation home?

Frequently, a family has a vacation home, lake cabin, beach house or some other place used by the family. It's where the kids grew up and where all of those childhood memories of summers on the lake or river were made. It's where the kids learned to swim, ski, and hunt. They built their first forts and campfires there—memories that still bring smiles to their faces today. Feelings about these places run deep and strong and I am frequently asked how to preserve the vacation home for the children.

The answer is not a simple one. In fact, there is no good answer, which is disappointing to many who want to preserve the family memory maker. Having dealt with these situations for many years, I believe the best thing to do is give the beloved vacation home to just one child instead of having the ownership shared among all children. The pitfalls of joint ownership greatly outweigh the advantages. While Mom and Dad are living, it all works just fine. They are in charge and they pay for all of the taxes, maintenance, and upkeep; they fix things when they break, set the rules, and can discipline a child and his family, if warranted. But everything changes after Mom and Dad are gone.

I met with a son who had just lost his parents. He was appointed Personal Representative of his mother's estate and told me there were four children, including him, and they were all in agreement about the family lake cabin.

"We want to keep the lake cabin for a family vacation spot," he said.

I nodded. "I understand, but I must warn you, it is not as easy as you think. For instance, if you four children jointly own the property, then each of you are personally liable for any injuries occurring on the property. You can keep insurance on the place to limit the exposure but you are still personally liable. Then there are the taxes due each year. Every one must pay his or her fair share and someone must do the collecting. What if one of you is short of funds that year? It might be the one brother who uses the cabin most often who can't pay his share of the taxes. Let's say he's having some money problems. One of his kids knocks the screen door off the hinges or breaks a window and it just sits there, un-repaired because he doesn't have the money to fix it. Then you discover the roof needs new shingles. You know this brother doesn't have the money to help pay for the shingles. The rest of you offer to purchase the shingles and let him do the work for his contribution, but he declines because he says he can't spare the time. He has time to go to the camp, but doesn't have time to put on the shingles. It's not long before the place starts to look like a dump and you are now embarrassed to bring your friends. But it doesn't matter because this brother is there every time you want to go. And it gets worse. Because of his financial problems, a tax lien is filed against the brother that immediately ties up the property. That means everyone else will have to contribute, again, and the only hope you have of forcing him to pay is to sue him. And those are just some of the problems I've seen over the years with jointly owned, family vacation homes."

"What if we take some of the money from the estate and establish a lake cabin account? Then we could have money to pay for the repairs and other expenses."

"How much do you set aside in this account? Remember, this brother doesn't have much money. You might be taking money from him that he needs to put his kids through school. And what happens if one of you gets divorced? You may end up owning the cabin with an ex-spouse. The problems increase if one of you dies suddenly. The spouse or kids inherit that one-quarter share. If your brother has 10 kids they each now own one-tenth of his share, but all have equal access to the property. If any of them run into tax problems, the IRS can force a sale. And if one of those kids decides they want to sell, but no one agrees to buy them out, they could force a sale through a legal partition action.

"What about a corporation?" he asked, "I've heard that a corporation may solve some of these problems."

"A corporation may solve some of these problems," I said. "The corporation will own the property, so any property liability will not spill over to you personally. The corporation bylaws could also set the schedule for use, maintenance, and repairs and even assess penalties for non-compliance. If financial contributions are required, the bylaws could outline how and when they are to be made. If not made, the bylaws could establish a plan for share forfeiture. The corporation could issue shares that are non-assignable and couldn't be taken by creditors or in a divorce. It could establish a plan for a share buy-out if one sibling wanted to sell."

"That sounds great—just what we need."

"If that's your decision, you will need to hold a family meeting to establish the bylaws of the corporation. You will need to establish a corporation and pay the filing fees. You will need funds to pay the yearly corporate filing fees and file a yearly tax return. Your accountant can advise you on that. If you need to vote on an issue, you will need to hold a shareholder meeting and vote. You can agree on what happens to the shares when one of you dies."

"Gee," he said. "That sounds like a lot of time, expense, and effort."

"It is, but someone must be in control and get the ball rolling. You've got to get together and establish the ground rules to put in the by-laws. Someone must collect the money for the fees and get the corporation established."

"Okay. I will get this started and call you when we are ready to go forward."

We shook hands and he left. I never heard from him again.

Legal Analysis: *There is no easy way to own a family vacation home after Mom and Dad have passed away. Many families may do well with the second generation (the children), but as they begin to die the problems will increase as the number of owners increases. It can lead to a real mess—within a generation no one will remember why they decided to keep the vacation home in the first place. It can easily lead to a split in the family because cousins are not as close as brothers and sisters.*

Keep car titles separate

Most couples title all of their assets jointly, although couples with large estates may separate their assets for inheritance tax planning. However, all couples, regardless of the estate size, should keep their car titles separate.

The separation of car titles is a way to protect assets. If the husband owns the car and runs into a bus and kills half the occupants, the resulting lawsuits will certainly be in excess of the auto policy liability limits. The owner and driver of the car, the husband, would be named in the lawsuits and it's possible his creditors could get half of the assets of the joint estate. However, if the car is jointly titled, the husband and wife would both be sued and creditors would be able to get most of the family assets except for the protected assets such as the homestead (in Florida and Texas) and retirement accounts such as the 401(k)s, IRAs, Keogh Plans, and SEPs.

A recent example…

A very nice older couple attended one of my seminars on estate planning and made an appointment to see me in my office. When I met with them I found their estate was worth a little more than $800,000. That included a house with a value of $175,000 and a mortgage payable to them of about $150,000. They had $250,000 in various qualified retirement accounts such as an IRA and 401(k) and another $150,000 in non-qualified investments (in this case, a Merrill Lynch brokerage account). They owned a lot which had an estimated value of $100,000.

I suggested they establish a Joint Living Revocable Trust, which would avoid probate and guardianship, and provide long-term protection for children and grandchildren. It's important to remember that a Living Revocable Trust is not an asset protection device—it will not protect assets from creditors. If you can get to your assets, which you can with a Living Revocable Trust, so can your creditors. I also suggested they re-title their vehicles with the husband's car in his name only and the wife's car in her name only. I noticed the wife wrote this advice down on a small blue post-it sticky note and placed it in their Trust book.

Two years later, these same clients were back in my office for a review of their estate plan. The wife looked a little stressed and the husband had dark circles under his eyes. I wondered if she was suffering from a terminal illness. It turned out they had been in a serious car accident. While driving on the interstate, they sideswiped a car, which swerved across the median and struck another vehicle head-on. Both drivers were killed and my clients were at fault. Their insurance will pay $100,000 per person with a maximum of $300,000 per accident where three or more are injured. In this case, the insurance company will tender its limits of $200,000 and be done.

Clearly, the liability exposure for this couple is well in excess of their insurance liability limits. The house is protected by Florida Homestead and their retirement accounts are also protected. Their other assets, however, are at risk because they had not re-titled their vehicles.

Unfortunately, asset protection must be done before the serious accident occurs. Any transfer of assets in an attempt to protect the estate after the accident will be ignored or treated as a fraudulent transfer of assets. Each state has its own set of Fraudulent Transfer Statutes or Codes. Although their house and IRAs were protected, this couple still had $200,000 at risk. Had they followed my advice, most of this unprotected money would have been safe. It's bad enough that they will have to bear the burden of knowing they were responsible for the loss of two lives, but in addition, their financial security is now in jeopardy.

Living Will — the last kind word

The Living Will gives a dying person the last word on when their life should end. One of my clients had a very ill sister, Missy. Missy's husband and son were with my client on the last day of Missy's life. The doctor called them all together and explained that Missy was being kept alive by the lung and heart machines and showed no signs of any brain activity. With no hope of recovery, the Doctor wanted permission from my client and Missy's husband to pull the plug to end her life. My client and her brother-in-law agreed.

My client has always felt uncomfortable about this decision because she gave permission to terminate her sister's life. If Missy had signed a Living Will, then she would have made the decision herself, ahead of time, sparing the family much pain. The rest of the family, including my client, would have been consulted by the doctor about the termination but would not have been the sole authorization for the termination of Missy's life.

Legal Analysis: *Following is an example of the language in a living Will:*

LIVING WILL
OF
JAMES SMITH

TO MY FAMILY, MY PHYSICIAN, MY LAWYER, MY CLERGYMEN
TO ANY MEDICAL FACILITY IN WHOSE CARE I HAPPEN TO BE:
TO ANY INDIVIDUAL WHO MAY BECOME RESPONSIBLE FOR MY HEALTH WELFARE OR AFFAIRS:

****

Death is as much a reality as birth, growth, maturity and old age — it is the one certainty of life. If the time comes when I can no longer take part in decisions for my own future, let this statement stand as an expression of my wishes while I am still of sound mind.

I, **James Smith**, willfully and voluntarily make known my desire that my dying not be artificially prolonged under the circumstances set forth below, and I do hereby declare:

If at any time I should have a terminal condition, an end-state condition or I am in a persistent vegetative state and if my attending or treating physician and another consulting physician have determined that there is no reasonable medical probability of my recovery from such condition, I direct that life-prolonging procedures be withheld or withdrawn when the application of such procedures would serve only to prolong artificially the process of dying, and that I be permitted to die naturally with only the administration of medication or the performance of any medical procedure deemed necessary to provide me with comfort, care or to alleviate pain.

In the absence of my ability to give directions regarding the use of such life-prolonging procedures, it is my intention that this declaration be honored by my family and physician as the final expression of my legal right to refuse medical or surgical treatment and to accept the consequences for such refusal.

I understand the full import of this declaration, and I am emotionally and mentally competent to make this declaration.

DATED: _______________.

____
James Smith

The declarant is known to me, and I believe him or her to be of sound mind.

____
Witness

____
Witness

Copies of this request have been given to:

They won't cash my check

Mom died leaving an estate and two sons. One son hired me to probate the estate. He wasn't sure where his brother was living. I was unable to locate him until I hired a private investigator. The P.I. gave me the address: Brevard County Jail, Titusville, Florida.

I called the jail in Titusville and located Bill. I said, "You don't know me but I'm a lawyer in Fort Walton Beach, and I've been hired by your brother to probate your mother's estate."

"So," he responded.

"Well," I said, "You are entitled to an inheritance from your mother's estate. The only asset is a rental house and we need to sell it so the estate proceeds can be divided." Now he seemed interested.

"You mean I'll get some money?" he said.

"I don't know how much, but yes, there will be some cash coming to you. Before you get it, though, you need to sign a deed."

He hesitated, and then with the conviction of one newly empowered, said, "I don't want to do no signing until I get out of jail. I need you to bond me out." He then explained he was in jail for non-payment of child support. He owed about $16,000 in back child support and needed $800 to bond out of jail and another $100 for bus fare to Fort Walton.

After about five weeks, we were able to arrange to do the closing sale of the house. Bill grudgingly agreed to sign the deed in jail and then sent the signed copy to my office. I presented it at the closing only after the closing agent handed me three checks: one for the back child support, one to bond him out of jail, and one for bus money back to Fort Walton Beach. We sent the money Federal Express. Several weeks later, Bill called my office and said he was in Fort Walton Beach. He wanted to know when he would get the rest of his money. His brother, as Personal Representative, controlled the money and was still tending to the estate bills. I told him it would be another several weeks before he got his money. He had nowhere to stay and no money, so he slept in the woods. He called my office every other day asking about his money and after about three weeks it finally arrived. When he called, I said the check was in my office so he said he would be "right" down to get his check. He arrived in a yellow cab and strolled into my office, shirtless. He had a tattoo, from what appeared to be a third grade artist, that said "Up yours Bitch," on his chest. His jeans were filthy because he had been sleeping in the woods for over three weeks. He only had three teeth and desperately needed a bath.

"Thanks for getting me my money," he said, as I handed him a check for $9,987.25. "All I want to do now is get my teeth fixed, get a bath, get glasses, and sleep in a real bed."

I said, "I will call ahead so the bank knows you are coming. You do have I.D., don't you?"

"Yes," he replied, and held up a Florida Driver's license.

As he left I said, "Good luck. I hope you get that bath."

He smiled and said, "So do I." My office staff was relieved to see him go.

Unfortunately, about 25 minutes later he walked back in my office to the surprise of everyone and said, "They won't cash my check."

"What's the matter?" I asked.

He showed me his driver's license and said, "They won't cash my check because my driver's license is expired. I've been in jail on and off for several years so I haven't needed one."

I called the bank and they confirmed their policy required a valid driver's license to cash a check. I tried to pressure them, but to no avail.

He said, "All I want to do is fix my teeth, get glasses, get a bath, and sleep in a real bed." He said he wanted to go to a check-cashing store and cash his check. I called one near my office and was told it would cost Bill 3.5% of the total check. That amounted to about $350.

Bill said, "I don't care, I just want to cash my check." He left my office a second time, again to the relief of my staff.

About 15 minutes later he was back. He said, "They won't cash my check."

"Why not?"

"They said it's not a regular check. It's from an estate account where there are only ten checks. Besides that, the guy there said he doesn't keep that much cash at the store."

He looked at me expectantly and said, "All I want is to get my teeth fixed, get glasses, get a bath, and sleep in a nice bed."

I asked him, "Is there any reason you can't get a new driver's license or an official Florida ID?"

"No, my criminal problems are not related to driving."

I handed him one of my white starched shirts I got back from the dry cleaners that day and five bucks for the ID and said, "Now I'm giving you the shirt off my back so you can go get an ID and get your check cashed."

He took my shirt, thanked me again and left my office for the third time.

Before my staff could tell me how relieved they were, Bill walked back into my office.

I said, "You've only been gone five minutes."

He nodded in agreement. "The Driver's License office is closed. It's Monday. All I want to do is cash my check so I can get my teeth fixed..."

"And get a bath and sleep in a bed. I know, I know," I interrupted. "Look, here's what we are going to do." I asked the lady cabbie who was driving him around to come in my office.

I said, "I'm going to write a check to this lady for $150. She has a license, so she can cash the check. She can pay herself for her time driving you around. The rest of the money will pay for a motel so you can get a bath and sleep in a bed. Then tomorrow morning she can pick you up so you can get a new Florida ID and cash your check. He smiled that three-tooth-grin. I will never forget it. At that point, I didn't care if I ever got my $150 back. He left for the fourth time. We locked and bolted the door.

The next day, about 11:30 a.m., I got a call on my cell phone. It was Bill. He muttered, "They won't cash my check."

I was too stunned to speak.

He said, "I just spent two hours down at the Driver's License office and got a new Florida ID. Then I went to the Bank and gave them my new ID and my check. They looked at the check and said they won't cash it because it was written for 5 cents more than was in the account."

Apparently, the brother wrote the check for $9,987.25, when the account held only $9,987.20.

I told him, "Stay where you are and I'll get right back to you." I called the bank and after a few choice words told them I would give them the 5 cents. The bank manager apologized, and said they would honor the check. I got back with Bill and said, "Take the check back to the bank and they will honor it."

He took it back and the bank honored it. That's the last time I spoke to Bill. However, he did stop by my office after cashing the check and gave my secretary the $150 I lent him.

I saw the cabbie seven months later. She relayed that Bill purchased several small gifts for friends in repayment for their kindness. He bought a cheap car, several new shirts, and a new pair of jeans. He got an apartment. He was very frugal with his money but never got a job. She said he ran out of money after about five months and she heard he was back in jail for petty theft. If he makes the proper requests, he can probably get a new pair of glasses and get his teeth fixed in jail. I know he is sleeping in a comfortable bed.

Two Generations

The clients

Many of my clients started working when they were fifteen to twenty years old, and they worked hard, taking any job that would put bread on the table. In the late 1930's and 40's, many of my clients, then eighteen years old or so, joined the services and fought in WWII. They were "real men" by the time they reached the age of nineteen or twenty. They were responsible adults (unlike many of today's twenty-year-olds, who are still living at home, getting an allowance). My clients lived during the depression and experienced its life-altering hardships. It changed their lives forever and deeply ingrained certain habits in them. They sacrificed, suffered, and did without so that they might accumulate money, just in case the bad times returned.

A lifetime of frugality left many with significant assets. Almost always without exception, they tell me, "Yes, we have a house and it's paid for." They remember how homes and farms were foreclosed during the depression. Most houses are valued between one hundred thousand and three hundred thousand dollars. Many clients have savings accounts, CDs, a brokerage account, and an extra parcel of land. Their qualified accounts, like IRAs and 401(k)s, account for twenty-five percent of their assets. Some clients with long-term employment at a large traditional company (like G.E., Exxon, or Southern Company) may have seventy to eighty percent of their estate assets held in their qualified accounts.

Most made money the old fashioned way—they earned it, and then they saved it. Ten years ago, most of my clients who had estates in excess of one million dollars made it in real estate. They invested in rental houses, land, or mobile home parks. They managed the properties over the years, cleaning up other people's messes; fixing broken pipes and unstopping toilets. After years of paying off mortgages and struggling financially, their investment finally paid off. They sold all of the properties and now live off the interest income. When the properties are sold, they pay the capital gains tax on the growth and depreciation recapture of twenty-five percent of the amount they depreciated. They grumble about the tax, but there is no denying their life is easier and more manageable. They have loads of dough and can enjoy the fruits of their labor.

But within the last seven years, more of my clients have become millionaires by long-term investing in the stock market. This strategy saw yearly portfolio increases of twenty to forty percent. It doesn't take many years, with a twenty percent return, for a modest investment to double and triple. Many portfolios valued at $400,000 in 1995, are now worth in excess of one million dollars today. This is true even with the collapse of the technical stocks and the bursting of the Internet bubble. Investment portfolios for most of my clients were conservative and contained only a small percentage of the risky hyper-growth stocks that generated all those negative headlines.

Long-term marriages

After several preliminary questions, I like to ask my client couple how long they have been married. I usually get two big smiles as they tell me thirty-five to fifty years or more. Most clients married as teenagers or in their early twenties. Times were different then and it was common to marry at an earlier age. Husbands were usually two to four years older than their wives, although I have seen a number of older women married to younger men. The age gap, in these instances, is usually five years or greater. I have read that this age gap occurs because the older woman wants to dominate the younger man, which may be true in the beginning. However, after thirty or forty years, they treat each other like anyone else and I usually find most men quite loyal and devoted husbands, regardless of the age gap.

Very few of my male clients are in a second marriage or show up with a much younger "trophy wife." If there is a second marriage, it too is usually long-term—fifteen to thirty-five years. One recent client of mine, a widower who was ninety-seven years old, married eleven years ago, when he was eighty-six. His bride was ten years younger and this was his second marriage. He was lonely and she needed the security, so it was a good match.

Over the last twelve years, I have done approximately three thousand Trusts and an additional four to five hundred Wills, but only a few of my clients have divorced. If a divorce occurs, I revoke the original Trust and then create two new Trusts. With a fifty percent divorce rate, one would think I would have a great repeat business, but I don't. Most of my clients are in long-term marriages and divorce is not an option. Art Linkletter once asked a female guest, "Have you ever thought of divorce?" She replied, "Divorce no; murder, yes!!" That sums it up. Most of my clients would not terminate their marriages. I would say that out of three thousand clients, perhaps four or five have been divorced, so the odds are pretty good that most of my clients will remain married until death.

Death brings up an interesting observation. Some of the most devoted and loving husbands will remarry quickly after the death of their wife, which often shocks their kids. Some understand, but most have a hard time accepting a quick remarriage. A devoted and loving husband will be more likely to quickly remarry because he loved his wife, depended on her a great deal, and is terribly lonely. Many of my widower clients say the crushing loneliness is too much for them to bear and a good man usually finds companionship fairly quickly.

Women, on the other hand, take two different paths. Women left with little financial security will often seek a new husband. If the woman is left financially secure, she will most likely replace her lost husband with a good dog. The dog provides company but is a lot less work. This is the age-old difference between the sexes. Women want security and men want companionship.

A lifetime of working and saving

Few clients report that they inherited money from their parents. Most of my clients never received an inheritance, but many now pay for their parent's current expenses. My clients acquired their assets during a lifetime of working and saving. Several clients invested in or invented something that made it big. One invented certain parts of the modern ceiling fan. Another invested in a company where she worked; it started as a small computer programming company, but now her shares are worth millions of dollars. Only two of my clients have won the lotto. In my experience, the chances of this happening are about the same as getting struck by lightning.

This trend regarding the inheriting of money is changing. Often, my clients tell me they expect to pass down very large inheritances—from several hundred thousand dollars to several million dollars. Within the next ten years, the amount of money expected to pass from the oldest generation to the next generation is estimated to be ten to twelve trillion dollars. This is more money changing hands in one generation than has changed hands in the entire history of our country. In the next twenty-five years, as much as one hundred trillion dollars will be passed to the next generation. This wealth transfer is unprecedented, and with the near elimination of the estate inheritance tax, it will be even more significant. Hundreds and thousands of kids in the next generation will receive millions of dollars they had no part in creating. Unfortunately, most will not have much money left in ten years, unless the inheritance is so great that it would take several lifetimes to spend. There will be a growing market for planning experts like me to guide families on how best to protect their children from themselves, and from too much affluence.

Comfortable, not extraordinary salaries

Many of my clients served in the military or the civil service. Others worked for big firms but were not CEOs. They were sales managers, marketing directors, even secretaries. Some were scientists and engineers or other professionals. Frequently, a client was self-employed. They owned a motel or a small business, or invested in real estate. I have yet to meet a Michael Eisner or a Bill Gates. My clients had incomes that were comfortable but not extraordinary. They paid their bills each month and had a little extra to invest for their future. Now they have reached that stage in life where they are no longer trying to make it to the next level. They realize they are not going to be rich millionaires, hobnobbing with jet setters. They are comfortable with their station in life and are financially and emotionally secure.

Two or three children

Like most Americans, my clients fit the national profile of having an average of two to three kids. Some have four or more, and I do have a few with seven and eight children. Most of my clients' children are in their late 20's to mid-50's, and most turned out fairly well. What I mean is that most are married (some more than once) and have good jobs and nice families. Few are as successful as their parents, although this number seems to be increasing. If they have more than one child, there is usually one "problem" child. This child has either not "found himself" or has some other difficulty. Problem areas seem to be drugs, drinking, depression, being a spendthrift, or just having a significant lack of common sense. Many of my clients believe their children's houses are too big, their cars are too expensive, and they spend way more than they should. Most clients are aware of this because they are tapped on a regular basis to financially bail out their kids.

Conservative Republicans

My law practice is limited to the panhandle of Florida, which is a very conservative area. I can count on one hand the number of Democrats I have encountered. Either there are no affluent Democrats, or they just don't tell me. Most clients vote in every election, are very patriotic, and have done at least some military service. I have had the privilege of talking to several war heroes who live in this area and have heard some incredible stories. Not long ago, I was discussing estate planning with a retired Air Force officer. During WWII, he flew bombing missions over Germany. After the meeting, I said, "I want to thank you for what you did for this country and me during the war. I really appreciate it." He looked at me for a long moment, and then replied "You're welcome." He probably hasn't been thanked in a long time, if ever.

My clients are very conservative. Their politics are conservative, their values are conservative, and their spending habits are conservative. They may have four hundred thousand dollars in a brokerage account, but they still drive a ten-year-old car. Almost always without exception, they own their homes free and clear. Few have any debts, other than mortgages, and they always look for the best deal when shopping. They ask for their senior citizen discount and are still concerned about saving money.

They have built a lifetime of spending habits that can't be changed. They can afford to take trips and enjoy the things their money can buy, but they don't. They are still trying to save and cannot bring themselves to spend money in what they regard as frivolous ways. They have no real desire to enjoy their affluence. In fact, few consider themselves affluent. They laugh when I tell them they have more money than 98% of Americans. Even if they are in their late seventies, their biggest concerns are running out of money and not having enough for their old age. They are concerned about being dependent upon their kids or the government. "What about medical bills? What about the nursing home?" they ask.

I tell them, "You have two million dollars and plenty of insurance; you will never run out of money. Why not enjoy yourself? Buy a motor home, take a trip, get a new car." They say they will, but I know they won't. It's too late for them to change a lifetime of spending habits. Of course, their kids will certainly enjoy the money their parents have scrimped and sacrificed to save for over forty or fifty years, but the money will probably be gone in ten years. The parents realize this but say, "At least it's better than giving it to the government." Someone is going to get it and it might as well be their children, even if they squander it.

Average age 65-75

My average client is between sixty-five and seventy-five years of age. For many, this is the first time they have really given any serious thought to estate planning. Over the years they may have had several simple Wills drafted. There are even some who have never had a Will. In the United States, according to the American Bar Association, 70% of our citizens do not have a Will. Generally, there are two triggering events that prompt a person to see me. The first being retirement. Most successful business people work hard and take their jobs seriously. Who has time to see a lawyer about dying and getting paperwork drawn up? After retirement, things slow down a bit and priorities shift. Taking care of personal business now becomes a top priority. The second event that brings clients to my office is the loss of a parent or close relative. They see first hand what havoc is caused by no planning and they want to avoid this mess for their own families.

Some don't think about Wills and estate planning. As long as their parents are alive, the parents act as a mental barrier against death. They can't die because their parents are still living. There is a natural order of things and some don't think about planning until after the loss of a parent. On several occasions, when seeing someone about their parent's estate, the client will say, "When this is over, I'd like to talk to you about my own Will and estate." But because parents are still living, they put off their own estate planning. My client's parents are usually eighty-five to ninety when they die, so that puts my clients at fifty-five to seventy-five with no planning of their own.

My clients tend to live longer than the average person. Very few smoke, they eat healthy foods, they are health conscious, and they get regular exercise. They have good medical insurance and see their doctor on a regular basis. Most of my clients have a good chance of living to see their 90th birthday. It's been my experience that if someone makes it past seventy-five or so and still has their wits intact, they will probably make it into their nineties.

I have very few clients in the twenty-five to forty age range. They may have printed a Will from a computer program and named their spouse as the beneficiary and the kids as the contingent beneficiaries. Unfortunately, most young couples make the same mistake. They don't see themselves as having a large estate needing estate planning. But many young couples are poor in assets but loaded in insurance. They may have five hundred thousand to one million dollars between them, which is a sizable estate and their simple Internet Will is woefully inadequate. It doesn't provide long-term protection for their kids. It may name a guardian but that's it. If the Will is a simple one, without a Trust, then the kids get all of the money when they turn eighteen (twenty-one in some states). By law, in most states, the money must be given to them with no strings attached and maturity (or lack of same) is not a factor. What they plan to do with the money is not a consideration. They could be drug addicts, alcoholics, or totally irresponsible and the money could ruin their life. The law provides no protection for kids over the age of eighteen when the parents have failed to prepare a proper estate plan.

If the Will doesn't provide for the creation of a Trust (called a Testamentary Trust), then a formal guardianship must be established. This entails guardianship plans, fees, reports, and never-ending court involvement. In some cases, this may be good. In others, it is a pain in the rear. Another problem occurs with young couples who, even if they establish some type of Trust in their Will, probably have not examined their beneficiary designations on their life insurance policies and deferred annuities (e.g., IRA, 401(k)). They usually name their spouse and then their children. Again, the kids are second to the spouse. Even if the Will establishes a Trust, the Will and Trust cannot control the assets passed directly to a minor child by way of a beneficiary designation. I have advised several young clients to name their "estate" as the beneficiary, so the money is always equally and fairly divided and held by the Testamentary Trust.

Wives at home

Most of my clients fit the typical 1950's stereotypes. The husband went off to work and the wife stayed home and took care of the children. Some wives held jobs early in their marriage, but most did not work outside the home. This trend is obviously changing. More and more wives now work outside the home and are proud of their contribution to the family budget. In some cases, wives actually make more money than their husbands. On two recent occasions, I've met with men who were house-husbands with wives who were the primary breadwinners. In each case, the wife did a lot of traveling and the husband sacrificed his job to be with the children. While this trend may be increasing, I don't expect to see the number of house-husbands and housewives becoming equal. I think the maternal instinct will prevail. Women may work, but their primary job during the childbearing years will be to take care of the children.

Since the 1960's, there has been a dramatic shift in the workforce. With the costs today of houses and cars, both parents will usually choose to work. A young couple may try to get their finances under control so that the wife can quit and stay home and take care of the children, but I have yet to see a couple trying to get to a financial level where the husband can quit his job so he can stay home and take care of the children.

College educated

Most of my clients, even the extremely elderly ones, are college educated. They are now retired military officers, business executives, or other retired professionals. Some had careers in management, sales, marketing, or a technical field such as chemical engineering. There are some who made their money in real estate; others made it as successful farmers. The farmers didn't make their money from farming. They made it because the land they own (occasionally thousands of acres) is now worth far more than the few dollars an acre their parents or grandparents paid for it.

Several of my clients have advanced degrees, including doctorate degrees, medical degrees, and legal degrees. The physicians I have seen are a mixed bag. Some are worth far less than you would imagine. In fact, some have saved so little they can never retire. The younger physicians are contributing heavily to their qualified plans (401(k), SEP, etc.), which will create a big nest egg for retirement unless they get divorced. Sometimes the doctor marries in medical school and the wife works and puts him through school. Then, when the doctor starts making big money, he dumps her for a young nurse. The wife gets the kids, alimony, half the assets, and plenty of child support. These payments can cut a doctor's net worth by more than sixty percent, which leaves him little chance for an early retirement. My advice to doctors is not to get married in medical school. Wait until you are older and get yourself a permanent trophy wife. To the women that marry doctors, I would say, keep yourself fit and your husband satisfied (which sounds like a sexist comment, and probably is. Come to think of it—there are many new female doctors).

Female doctors present a unique set of circumstances. They are the major breadwinners and sometimes the man is the house-husband. Who gets the kids and how much alimony is paid are issues I have not dealt with yet. Does the female doctor/wife fool around with a male nurse or does the house-husband fool around with the neighbor's wife? With a fifty percent divorce rate, the answers should soon be forthcoming.

Frugal spenders

My clients who were born before 1917 are very interesting. Not only have they experienced two World Wars, but they lived during a time of great affluence-the 1920's. Jobs and money were plentiful and it was a great time for most. Then the Depression came. It destroyed lives and fortunes; lifestyles changed overnight. Banks collapsed and an entire generation lost faith in financial institutions. Ten years of Depression will do that. They learned to save money for the bad times and to make sure their investments were safe and conservative. Many of my clients have two or three hundred thousand dollars in CDs or saving accounts. Although many clients did not trust brokerage firms for a long time after the 1929 Stock Market Crash, most have gone back to the brokerage firms because their investments are too much to handle without a monthly account statement.

After a lifetime of saving and sacrifice, many of my clients' nest eggs have grown enormously. Many have five hundred thousand to one million dollars in cash, yet they still can't bring themselves to take that dream vacation or buy that car they always wanted. Their behavior is now automatic and they can't change. They will never really enjoy their money, but their kids certainly will.

Clients born from 1920 to 1935 fall into a similar mold. They were part of the depression but may not have fully experienced it. For example, my mother was born in 1933, but then did not understand the impact. As a little girl, she thought it was normal to travel from town to town with her parents as they looked for work. Some nights the meals were not very fancy, but everyone else was doing the same thing so she thought it was normal. As a young child, she learned to be thrifty and conservative because it was so important to her parents.

The next generation—the Baby Boomers—is a mixed bag of very frugal and very liberal spenders. Some pinch pennies and some don't. The generation following the Boomers, Generation X, those born between 1965 and 1976, is one of very liberal spenders. The thought of turning out a light, saving used foil, and washing a plastic cup is completely foreign. They just spend and charge until their credit is cut off, then file bankruptcy and start over again.

Most of my clients will retain their estate assets until the occurrence of one of three events. The first is suffering an extraordinary medical problem not covered by insurance. But this is rare. Most of my clients have very good insurance, but a catastrophic illness could exceed medical coverage.

The second event is the need for a nursing home. This is the most likely occurrence that can wipe out an estate. After the age of sixty-five, a person has a forty-three percent chance of needing a nursing home. After the age of seventy, the likely-hood increases to fifty percent. The average cost of a nursing home in 2005 is $5,000 to $6,000 per month. This is $60,000 to $72,000 per year of cash assets needed to pay this expense. Even after scrimping and sacrificing for fifty years, most family budgets can't generate enough income to pay for the nursing home cost without dipping into principal. When both Mom and Dad are in a nursing home at the same time, the cost can be financially devastating for all but the largest estates.

The third event involves an interloping neighbor or unscrupulous family member coming in and grabbing the estate at the last minute (changes are made to the Will in the last six months of life). This is commonly referred to as the "swoop and scoop." A Will or Trust contest with lengthy and expensive litigation is needed to resolve the dispute. Legal fees amounting to 45% or more of the estate leave no one a winner.

Safe and sound

Most of my clients have never been sued or involved in a major personal injury accident, nor have they ever sued anyone—usually their only contact with attorneys comes from a child's divorce. Most of their opinions about lawyers come from newspaper articles, TV shows, and movies. When they meet an Estate Planning lawyer, like me, they say with surprise, "You're really a nice guy." Many ask if they can call me if other legal problems arise. I tell them I will refer them to the proper attorney for help if it's a problem I cannot handle. Although I limit my practice to one area—estate planning and probate—I know many top attorneys in other areas.

Early in my legal career, I did personal injury work, which usually involved car accidents, slip and falls, and product liability cases. As a result, I do have a sympathetic ear for the wrongfully injured. As I have said, most of my clients are very conservative. Many think injured people should not be allowed to sue, that attorneys are leaches (except for me, of course), and that personal injury awards are ridiculous. To give them another view of personal injury lawyers, I often pose the following scenario which is based on actual facts: I ask them to assume they are the only bread winner in the family and are in their car, stopped at a red light, minding their own business. A drunk driver, who is on suspension for drinking on the job, plows into the back of their car. They suffer three broken ribs and a spinal disc rupture, which puts them in the hospital for several weeks. Now partially disabled, they lose work and, ultimately, their job. Their family faces financial ruin and they will be in pain for the rest of their life. Although previously very active, they can no longer play tennis or golf or even pick up a grandchild. I ask the client what he would do. Interestingly enough, no matter how horrific I make the scenario, most tell me if they had to sue, it would only be for the medical bills and lost wages. No compensation for the loss of lifestyle or pain and suffering. No money for future loss of earning power and future medical bills, and no compensation for the total loss of enjoyment of life. They think they should live with the cards God dealt them because money will not replace what they lost.

I understand their reluctance. They come from a generation that took care of their own problems. They prided themselves on their independent spirit and avoided taking handouts from anyone. Receiving money above and beyond their bare expenses leaves a bad taste in their mouths. Occasionally, I can persuade them that it is not a sin to receive compensation that would make their lives a bit easier if they were badly injured—money to pay for pain management, physical therapy, or a motorized wheelchair—but it's usually an uphill battle. If I were a personal injury lawyer, I would not want one of my clients on their jury.

Father knows best

Most client homes are the typical "Father knows best" households where the husband is dominant. However, in later years, if the husband loses his mental abilities, the wife is forced to take over. Many women have relied upon their husbands to make all the important decisions. If dementia or Alzheimer's sets in, the wife may be helpless. But most women step up to the plate and take over. They learn how to handle the finances and make the major decisions. Some exact a certain retribution for being treated like second-class citizens over the years, but others are very caring and understanding and saddened by their husband's condition. The great and kind man they knew so well now can't remember where he parked the car.

Some wives who have never been given financial responsibilities have a hard time coping with this new duty and must rely on others. If she has decent children, she can lean on them. Otherwise, she may be on her own and has to learn about finances and how to manage the family budget by herself. I routinely suggest to couples that if the wife has never balanced the checkbook or managed the investments, she take on these tasks for at least two months. The husband should not write a check or help out, unless his wife has no solution to a problem. The wife will likely be taking care of all of the finances some day anyway, so why not let her start now when the husband is around to help and advise?

There are certain investment groups and women's organizations that provide information and support to recently widowed women. In addition to this, I often suggest that they sign up for a finance class at the local university or junior college so that they can educate themselves and not have to rely on someone else.

We don't want to be a burden

Many clients have paid their children's college tuition, bought them several cars, and paid the down payment for their first house. But in spite of this one-sided generosity, most parents do not want to be a financial burden on their children. To that end, many of my clients have eliminated this possibility by selling their homes and purchasing a unit at a retirement village. When more skilled care is needed, another apartment will be provided by the village and finally, when nursing care is needed, they will be moved to this unit. The cost is fixed and most financial arrangements are made up front so there is no uncertainty later. The difficult decisions about what to do with Mom and Dad and who will care for them are already made and the burden lifted from the children.

Unfortunately, most parents don't do this. Even though parents may not want to burden their children, their children are left with many difficult decisions. Since seventy percent of U.S. citizens do not even have a Will, it will come as no surprise that even fewer have a durable power of attorney. Often, this requires the children to make difficult decisions that can become a major burden for them. In my opinion, this burden is becoming a regular part of life, like death and taxes. You raise your children and when the last one has finally left the nest, you and your spouse are ready for the good life. You now have the free time to travel and enjoy the fruits of your life of hard work and sacrifice. Then you receive a call that your parent needs you to care for them. Not that many years ago, the life expectancy of a parent was seventy to seventy-five. Now many parents are living well into their nineties. In years past, they would die before they became your obligation. Now, with improved medical care, they are outliving their savings and planning. When they were growing up they did not plan for extreme old age. Few people think they will become incompetent or need to be placed in a nursing home, but many will. I see it every day.

Children may have to suddenly deal with making legal decisions for their parents either through a durable power of attorney or through a formal legal guardianship. They are also left with the second or third most stressful situation a person can face—making the decision to place a parent into a nursing home when they don't want to go. While most parents would not want a child to have to make such decisions, the lack of any planning can virtually guarantee the burden will indeed be placed on their children.

Good men remarry fast

I happened to be listening to Dr. Laura Schlesinger's radio talk show one afternoon when she told a caller it was common that good men remarried quickly after losing a wife. Many men were crushed after losing their wives. After many years in a long and loving relationship, they were very dependent upon their wives and the resulting loneliness was overwhelming. Some even hinted at ending their lives. None of my clients have ever done this and many have since remarried. Some remarried within a few months after the death of their wife, and others within a year or so, but it seemed the more loving and devoted the husbands, the quicker they remarried.

In a recent case, one of my clients was in grief counseling because he was so devastated by his loss. But just three months later he was married again…to the grief counselor! He told me, "She's not a 'looker,' but she does keep me company and I sure have been awful lonely." Some men take more time to remarry, and there comes a time and condition when most men just will not remarry because of age. Anna Nichole Smith may disagree with me, but there aren't many men who have a billion dollars.

After losing his wife, it may take a man some time to start dating again—he's a little out of practice. He may join a dance club, church group, or other senior organization. Often the "good friend referral network" swings into action and there are always plenty of amateur matchmakers available. There is also another source for potential mates: the widowed spouse of a best friend. For example, a couple meets another couple. They become great friends, travel together, and spend a lot of time in each other's company. Then one wife dies; later, the other couple's husband dies. The two remaining comfort each other and eventually get married, although there was never a physical relationship prior to that time. I have seen this on several occasions.

Another interesting event I have seen occurs when a spouse dies. The surviving spouse will make contact with a high school sweetheart and get married. Here's a recent example, although the couple has not married, yet. Apparently, they were each other's first sweethearts in high school. The woman was on a calling service informing the newly widowed husband of certain services offered by her senior group. They lived in the same town and they knew of each other but hadn't made contact for over 50 years.

After she called him, they had dinner and have been together ever since. When they started discussing estate planning, they found I had done legal work for both of them, before their spouses had passed away. I saw them recently at one of my workshops, sitting together, giggling like the high school sweethearts they had once been. The man looked great. He had spring in his step and was mentally sharp, though just a few months earlier he looked very old and frail. It just goes to show you how, at any age, a good woman will put starch in your pants.

A spiritual life

My impression after meeting many thousands of clients is that most are spiritual. They may be Christians, Jews, Muslims, Hindus, or some other group, or simply believe in God and worship Him in their own way. Many regularly attend worship services and are active members of a church. This spiritual confidence often seems to help them become successful in their work. I rarely see the maverick genius billionaires who are a breed all unto themselves. I see the family man and woman living a spiritual life, slowly accumulating assets. As they approach the end of their lives, they want to pass the family estate to their children with as little expense and with as few problems as possible. It's been my experience that many extremely successful men don't pay much attention to their spiritual concerns until they reach their mid-forties. After all their success, they are faced with the question, "What else is there?" Many find that God is still there and they turn to their church and family for strength. Others think that chasing younger women is the answer. They end up divorcing their wives and their children, and rarely find the peace and happiness that comes with a strong faith in God and family. Many of these will end up quite lonely, with many regrets.

Their children

About ninety percent of my clients have children. While many of their children are college educated, their graduation rate is actually lower than their parents. Some children are extremely successful, but many are still struggling financially and often have little in the way of accumulated assets. On the other hand, most children do have substantial term life insurance policies ($250,000 to one million dollars). This insurance provides for the spouse and children in the event of an untimely death and is not purchased to create wealth or pay inheritance taxes. Most children have financial problems because they want what their parents have and they want it right now. They don't understand the concept of delayed gratification, and they have not developed their parents' habits of frugality and thrift. They buy big houses with big mortgage payments. They buy the cars their parents always wanted, but could never afford. Their houses are filled with new furniture and electronic gadgets galore with everything financed, often on credit cards with crushing interest rates. And they wonder why they never have any extra money.

There are some children that have never made much of their lives. Even though they may be in their forties, their parents still help with their daily bills. Some parents pay off their child's credit cards because they find the interest rates appalling. They may also pay the house note or let the child live in a house for free. They want the child to have a nice house and know the child couldn't afford one on their own. They may also pay for a new car because they want the child to have reliable transportation.

These children and grandchildren are very active. The wife is often a typical soccer Mom transporting the children from one activity to another. The days are packed with school and extra-curricular school activities and the children are extremely busy. Most have a good relationship with their parents and try to include them in the grandchildren's activities. In my experience, daughters have a closer relationship with the parents than do sons.

Because the children of my clients are so busy with work, their children, and school activities, they quite naturally think more often about their children than they do about their parents. Of course, this will change if a parent suffers a major physical illness or needs nursing home care. Some children have seen the consequences of a lack of proper estate planning first hand, as friends endure a parent's mental decline or episode of serious illness. As a result, most children want their parents to do proper estate planning, in case the need arises. Proper planning on the parent's part goes a long way to reduce a child's already stressful life.

Most children encourage their parents to spend more money on themselves. They want them to take trips, buy that new car, or remodel the house. If the children get an inheritance down the road, that's nice, but it's rarely part of the child's financial planning. On the other hand, there are some children who don't want their parents to spend any money—they feel they are entitled to an inheritance and it's their money. They will go to great lengths to maximize their inheritance, which may include ensuring that their siblings are cut out of the Will or Trust and preventing a parent from remarrying. This type of child often splits the family apart and causes litigation.

Rarely have I ever seen the children abandon a parent in need. One or more of the children make their home available or spend extraordinary time taking care of a needy parent.

Average age of the children

Most of my clients' children are over the age of twenty-five years, with some in their fifties and sixties. One ninety-seven-year-old client told me "Yeah, my boy is now seventy-two." No matter what your age, you are still your parent's child. While most parents are proud of their children, when meeting with their lawyer they can be brutally honest. Even though a child may have had a successful career and is now retired, if the parent thought that child was selfish or not very thoughtful, the parent will tell me. When picking the personal representative or successor Trustee, they decide who will best perform the job. I usually suggest they pick the child who will be the most fair, not the one with the most business sense. If the children are all on equal footing, they may pick the oldest or the one who lives the closest.

College educated and away from home

Since most of my clients are college educated, they have tried to provide the same opportunities for their children, many of whom have gone to college as well. After college, many of their children have taken jobs in other cities. Few of my clients have children that live near them in the same city. Their college educated children have children and careers of their own and are very busy. Many try to call Mom and Dad on a regular basis, but many others do not. Too often a parent tells me, "My son never calls. He hooked up with a woman who controls him and he really has not been part of the family since their marriage." This is the child who will see his share of the estate reduced or eliminated. Keep in contact with your parents. They are the only ones you will ever have and they won't live forever. Time moves so fast. Your children grow up and move away and then your parents die. Just like that, they are gone.

When I reach an impasse with my son, I say, "I'm in my forties and a fairly smart guy. I am not doing this just for myself. My only goal is for you to have a great life—a life better than mine. You can do whatever you want, but I'm telling you the right thing to do is …" This works most of the time. Unfortunately, for many children, the only way they can learn a lesson is to suffer the consequences that follow a bad decision. If they don't show up at work, they get fired. Mom can't call in and lie for them so they can keep their job. Often, Mom can't pay their bills. The child must suffer and feel the emotional pain of not having anything before they pick themselves up and move on to a productive and prosperous life. In my opinion, the moms who continually cover, stop, and bail out their children deny them the opportunity to be successful.

You may have noticed that I only refer to "Moms." Most of the time it is the Mom who is the enabler, rarely the Dad. Women feel responsible for their children. They think it must have been something they did or didn't do when little Johnny was growing up that caused him to be the way he is. They don't really say this, but I know that's what they are thinking. Dads usually don't feel this way. They think once you are old enough, you are responsible for your own decisions. A dad can kick a kid out of the house; a mom usually can't.

Not as wealthy

Many children have very little savings and have accumulated few assets compared to their parents, but there are exceptions. Someone is buying those $500,000+ houses, those large boats, planes, and nice cars, and it's usually not the parents. Some children had the good luck to be in the right industry at the right time. Regardless of their level of employment success, most are not very savvy investors. Most of my client's children are so busy they have neither the time to cull the market for good stock picks, nor the extra money required to invest. That extra one hundred dollars probably went for a new pair of soccer shoes for one of their children.

Often my clients' children are doing fairly well, but they lack financial security and financial savvy. This causes concern for the parents who are afraid their children may not be able to handle an inheritance and will just blow all the money. In situations like this, I suggest they take the children for a financial test ride. Give the children some money now—eventually, they're going to get it all anyway—and see what they do with it. Usually, I suggest the parents establish a brokerage account with their broker titled in the name of the child. The parent maintains a presence but only as an investment advisor. This way, the parent can make suggestions and keep tabs on the account.

The account is set up and funded with several thousand dollars on a yearly basis. The child has a stake in the investment and now has a reason to learn about the market. It should be agreed that this money is for the child's retirement and can't be touched until age sixty-five. A regular gifting program over several decades can net hundreds of thousand of dollars for the child's retirement. There are many advantages to this test drive. The gifted amounts are excluded from the parent's estate for tax consideration. The children learn about the market. The children can become financially secure and aren't just waiting for Mom and Dad to die. If the child takes the money out of the account, the parent can take countermeasures, such as changing the estate plan to keep the child's money tied up in a Trust because it's now apparent they can't be trusted.

The first three thousand dollars of any gift should be set up as an IRA account. There are several benefits here. This gets an IRA started where none existed before. Further, the IRA gift is a direct deduction from the children's tax return. If the child made fifty thousand dollars, he can now report his income was only forty-seven thousand because three thousand dollars went to the IRA. It doesn't matter that the three thousand came from Mom and Dad. A gift is not income and does not have to be reported to the IRS.

Lots of life insurance

When you are young and healthy, life insurance is cheap. A healthy twenty-five year-old male can purchase a one million dollar policy, with level premiums for twenty years, for around forty dollars per month. If he dies, he leaves a one million dollar estate, which is sizable. If he dies, his wife and children are usually the beneficiaries. But if his wife dies in the same accident, then the children are the beneficiaries. With no planning, the State where you live determines who gets the money and when. If Mom and Dad die in a car accident and leave two children, say four and six years-old, the children get the money. The "State" doesn't get the money, but does control how the money is used and when it goes to the children. In this situation, if the deceased young couple didn't have a Will, the State would require a legal guardianship be established. Two guardians would be appointed to look after the interests of the children. If a family member is deemed suitable, that person might be appointed as guardian of the children and of the money. The court would restrict how and when the money could be used. So far, this doesn't seem so bad. The State usually requires that this money (which may well have grown to over a million dollars for each child) be held in the guardianship accounts and be given to the child at a certain time. As determined by the State, that time is when the child has reached the peak of intellectual maturity, knows everything, and is capable of making the most mature and logical decisions about what to do with their inheritance. That, of course, is when the child reaches the age of eighteen.

I am personally not aware of any young beneficiary who has kept the money very long or benefited in any meaningful way from a large inheritance. It is my opinion that there is nothing more destructive than giving a brain-dead eighteen year-old a wad of dough. They think they would look great in a Ferrari—until they have to pay the repair bills. Suddenly receiving a big chunk of money may derail a decent child. Instead of going to school and getting a degree, they decide to travel the world and have a good time. Why should they work for minimum wage when they have five hundred thousand dollars in the bank? Why should they put up with the boss's crap when they make more in interest income than he makes in salary? Most never learn how to work themselves up from the bottom. They never learn the value of overcoming adversity. Too much money at a young age is very destructive.

A simple Will with a Testamentary Trust could have saved the day. Most young adults don't need a Living Revocable Trust. This Trust is usually set up to avoid probate and guardianship. The Trust that most young adults need is created in their Will, and is called a Testamentary Trust. The Trust can make provisions for your children and will usually identify a Trustee of your choice to manage the money. The Trustee will be guided by the terms of the Trust and will pay all expenses such as living, school, college, and post-graduate studies. The funds can also be turned off until some pre-set date. Most will keep the checkbook out of the hands of the children until they are at least twenty-five years of age. I usually suggest moving this age to thirty or thirty-five. A few clients have moved this age to forty, fifty, or even sixty-five years. When the pre-selected age is reached, the Trustee turns over the accounts to the beneficiaries.

There is one critical element to this planning; the insurance must be payable to your estate. If you name your children as the beneficiaries on your life insurance policy, they get the money directly and immediately. If underage, a guardianship will be established and they'll get the money at age eighteen, even though your Will directs a Trust be established. Remember, a Will only controls the assets that go through probate. Your life insurance beneficiary gets the money directly from the life insurance company. The check is not controlled by your Will and Trust unless it is payable to your estate.

Most clients want their children to get a good education and be financially secure. If you provide money for a proper education and turn off the financial spigot until they retire, both goals are met. You haven't ruined them. You haven't created Trust bums, children who never make anything of their lives and don't contribute to society but exist month to month on the check they receive from Daddy's Trust.

Looking for fulfillment

In the days when my grandparents grew up (1910-1930), getting a job was a big deal. The job market was tight and any job that offered a reasonable amount of security and adequate pay was a "good" job. Often, people like my grandparents worked their entire careers in jobs they did not like. But they felt they had no choice because they had to support a family and jobs were scarce. If they ended up in a dead end job with little job satisfaction, that was just the luck of the draw.

Employment decisions have changed dramatically. Since then children today are looking for fulfillment. They want a job they like. They want a rewarding career where they make a contribution to society. Unfortunately, many children are immature and never figure out what they really want to do or be until they are in their late twenties. They flounder around for the first ten years, trying to "find themselves," trying different jobs to see which ones they like best. You can see the difficulty employers have when hiring young adults. They put time, effort, and money into training new employees—and then see them leave after six months.

It usually takes many different jobs and several career changes before children finally settle down and find a job they like. When they do start a family, it's usually ten years later than their grandparents. Many of my clients are deeply concerned about their children. The years are passing, but their children seem to be going nowhere. I tell them that times have changed and children today have the luxury of being able to try out many different jobs or career fields as they search for the job that gives them fulfillment. I ask my clients if they would have appreciated such an opportunity. Most agree it would have been nice to find a job they really enjoyed doing. The great majority of my clients are truly decent people who have raised decent children. The children may stray for a while, but in the end, the children will usually turn out to be just as decent as their parents.

One client of mine was really down on his son, who was his only child. The boy did well until he turned sixteen and Dad got him a car. Then the child got mixed up with a bad crowd and started doing drugs. He wrecked the car and was arrested several times for drug possession. Each time, his dad bailed him out and paid the bills. The child repeatedly lied and stole from his dad. On top of everything else, he did not go to college.

My client came from a generation that had an almost mystical reverence for higher education and this was a major blow. The dad told me this story as I was creating his Trust. In this Trust, Dad did not want this boy, now twenty-three, to get any money until he turned forty-five.

Seven years later, I went fishing with this same client and his son who was working as a first mate on a charter fishing boat. The boy loved to fish and was using part of his wages to buy into a charter fishing boat of his own. A year later, he was the captain of his own boat and very responsible. He started an IRA investment account and is now doing quite well. My client and I talked about the situation. He recognized that his son had matured and although he did not get a college education, he was doing what he wanted to do. This boy is happy to wake up every morning and loves to go to work. And why wouldn't he? He gets to fish every day and he even gets paid for it! (Where did I go wrong?) There are many examples of children like this who have a slow start but end up doing quite well. And besides that, this boy's parents have become his IRA retirement account. He will get more from them than he could ever save on his own. He knows his financial future is set, so why not enjoy life now?

Coddled

In one sense, children today grow up in a much more protected environment. In another sense, however, they grow up in a much more sexually-explicit environment. Moms and Dads protect their little ones from everything—except what Hollywood shows them.

Most children lead very structured lives. They wake up and prepare for school. They go to school and attend a different class every fifty minutes. When school is over, many participate in after-school activities or sports. Football, baseball, soccer, cheerleading, band, and all of the other after-school activities consume most of the remaining daylight hours. Once home, the children clean up, get a snack, and begin to study. Then comes dinner, and afterward another hour or so of study, and off to bed. Then up in the morning and off to another planned and highly structured day. This goes on five days a week, but many weekends are also consumed by more school activities. Once in a while, the child must do chores around the house, which takes another couple of hours. After this activity, the children will probably take a nap. The children are so busy they cannot get into trouble, which isn't a bad thing. When their parents were children, some of them goofed around and some got into trouble. But they learned from their mistakes and they learned—sometimes the hard way—about life. By the age of nineteen or twenty, these parents were supporting a family or fighting in a war. Most children today do not achieve the same level of maturity as their parents until they are well into their late twenties. Some parents tell me it's even later than that!

Every day I see children who know nothing about responsibility, duty, honor, honesty, and hard work. They live a protected and sheltered life and are given everything. Their parents do all they can to ensure that little Johnny or little Jane doesn't have bad experiences. If little Johnny turns a paper in late, the parent makes an excuse so he won't get a bad grade.

One of my high school teachers came to see me last year to do some estate planning. She taught high school for over thirty-five years but was no longer in the profession. I asked her what was the biggest difference she had noticed in the children she had taught over the years. She didn't hesitate for a moment and said that today's children have no respect for adults and their parents coddle them. She said she left teaching because she got tired of dealing with parents who constantly made excuses and took up for their children. If a child didn't turn in a paper or did a crappy job, she believed that his or her grade should reflect that lack of effort. But many parents would call and argue that a low grade would ruin their child's chances of getting into a good college. My teacher believed a student should turn in his work when it was due, like everyone else.

Believe me, this is a constant battle even at my house. I feel my children should sink or swim on their own. If they fail, they'll learn what it feels like to fail and they'll learn the consequences of not doing the work or turning it in on time. Isn't that the way life works? If you do a crappy job or turn in your work late, you can get fired. I would rather my children learn this in middle school and high school than when they are twenty-five and supporting a family. If my twenty-five-year-old son loses his job, he might have to move back in with us! I can tell you right now, I'll do everything in my power to make sure my children learn the necessary life lessons now so they can be successful later in life.

Nice house and cars. Very nice.

Many young adults are into material things. They did not live through the Depression and WWII. They don't know what it's like to worry about where their next meal is coming from because they have never truly been hungry. They are part of the self-centered "me" generation.

It's a great time to be alive. If you want something, why put it off until later, right? Get it now while you are still young and can enjoy it. Many of my clients say their children may live in a $250,000 house, but they have to help them pay the mortgage. Many of my clients end up paying off their child's credit card bills as well—$15,000 to $20,000 is not uncommon. The twenty-percent interest rate drives the Dad crazy so he dips into savings and pays off all the cards assuming the children have learned their lesson and will now cut up the cards and never use them again. But, of course, that doesn't happen. With a zero balance, many children soon max them out again. Many young adults (under forty) have a house full of things, but have no discipline and no concept of delayed gratification.

Help!

There is one way to share the family wealth and not spoil the children: help them buy a house. Assisting them with the down payment can make a big difference, since many young adults have a hard time saving money. The expense of raising children today is staggering and it's hard to save the ten or twenty percent needed to make that first down payment. Many parents come to the rescue with down payment money, which I think is a great idea. But I think paying for the entire house is a bad idea. I'd be concerned that the children might take the money that would have been spent on a house payment and use it to buy more "things." If Dad wants to help, and has the financial ability, let the children pay their own mortgage while Dad invests a like sum for their retirement. After twenty or thirty years, that could mean a huge nest egg for retirement.

On the go

My clients are often amazed at the lifestyles their grown children maintain. They are on the go seven days a week, carting the grandchildren from one activity to another. I have three children, and I know how active life can be. One spring, my wife had each of my sons involved in three different activities. One boy played on a soccer team, a baseball team, and a basketball team. The other son played on two baseball teams and a soccer team. Meanwhile, my daughter was dancing and playing T-ball. On a typical Saturday, I would leave at seven in the morning with one kid and my wife would leave with the other two. We would take the different game outfits with us and change in the car. At some point, we would usually meet and exchange children. The day would end at seven or eight that night, after six or seven games. Weekdays, with school and sports practice after school, was also very busy. There's no doubt that young families today are much busier than their parents ever were, but the level of involvement with their children is also much greater.

Warm relations

Although there are always exceptions, most of my clients' parents report they have a good relationship with their children. While their children are very busy with their own families, most seem to take time to stay in contact with Mom and Dad. Daughters are usually closer to their parents than sons. However, if a submissive daughter is in a relationship with a domineering man, the relationship can be strained. In this case, many parents want some strings attached to any money given to the daughter. Sometimes the parents will cut out the daughter completely—not to punish the daughter, but to ensure the bum son-in-law does not get his hands on the parent's money. They feel if their daughter got any money she would give it all to her worthless husband.

A more common scenario is the son is married to an overbearing wife. The son is the proverbial "whipped" man. Some of these women try to control the son, and the parents, by limiting the amount of time the grandparents can spend with the grandchildren. Eventually, the parents get fed up with this situation, so they ask me to change their estate plan. Often the son, and his wife, are left out of the parent's Will and Trust. Sometimes, the grandchildren are included, but often, they are left out as well.

Generally, I see the son drifting away unless he has a good wife. As a boy grows up, he usually has a special relationship with his mom, as any Mom will tell you. Then the son gets married and now has a new woman in his life. I think his first priority should be his God. Next, should be his wife, his children, and then his mother. Mom is now in forth place, but in her mind, her son is still in the top spot. A good daughter-in-law, who includes Mom in activities and remembers special occasions, can be a big help. I remember my mom's birthday, but it is my wife that keeps the communication channels open. If the Mom is neglected, her feelings will be hurt. If that happens, she may decide it's not the fault of her son but "that girl he married." The next thing that happens is that Mom, my client, shows up at my office and has me change her estate plan so the daughter-in-law won't get any of Mom's money. Parents think more often about their children than the children think about their parents, but it's a wise child who works to improve that ratio.

Many kids want parents to do estate planning

Most children want their parents to do some estate planning. They may not know what level of estate planning is needed, but they know it should be started. Some children are brought into the financial fold at that time. It's been my experience that about sixty percent of my clients don't mind discussing their estate with their children, while the remainder want to make sure their children know nothing about their estate. Of course I can accommodate my client's wishes either way; however, I strongly recommend that if a child is selected as successor Trustee, that he or she be given a copy of the Trust and instructions on what to do, ahead of time. After the Trust is established, I like to see the clients back in my office within six to eight months, with their children, to discuss the progress of their estate plan. These meetings are usually positive and productive. If everyone knows what to expect, and who is in charge, the chance for problems are greatly reduced. Good communication is usually the key to minimize family problems.

Most of my client's children want their parents to enjoy the fruits of their labor, but many parents have a hard time spending money on what they regard as an extravagance (e.g., a long trip or a new car) no matter how much their children prod them. After a lifetime of scrimping and saving, they can't break their frugal mindset. Mom feels guilty if she gets a new purse when she just saw a perfectly serviceable one at the church rummage sale for two bucks. I often tell clients they might as well try to have a good time with their money because their children certainly will.

A right to their parents' money

Some greedy children think they are entitled to their parent's estate, and some even think they get half when the first parent dies. Generally, these children are more concerned about what will be left rather than what is needed to provide care for the parent. Often they dominate the parent, preventing the parent from remarrying and deliberately disrupting any potential relationships. Several widowed clients have admitted they don't look for companionship because it would upset the children.

One client of mine, a widower about 70 years old, lived in a small concrete block house. He purchased this house with his wife 45 years ago, and it is currently worth about $50,000. He has $8,000 in a checking account and receives $1,200 a month in income, mainly from Social Security. He met with me to discuss his estate, which seemed to be pretty modest until he told me that he owned 400 acres of timberland in Georgia, worth almost $900,000. I asked him what he would do if he had an additional $900,000 in his checking account. His eyes brightened and he said, "I have always wanted to take a cruise, but I haven't had the money."

"If you sold some or all of that timberland, you'd have the cash to enjoy life a little more and maybe take that cruise."

He shook his head and said, "I can't sell the land. It's been in the family for three generations. Besides that, the children don't want me to sell the land."

I'm sure they don't, nor do they want him to remarry.

After a parent is lost

Mom passed away just a few months ago, and the children are still grieving the loss of Mom. How can Dad be dating already? Sometimes, these whirlwind romances surprise the rest of the family—maybe shock is a better word. To them, it seems like he is cheating on her, or at, least cheapening her memory. The children's feelings are hurt and they are outraged with Dad. Often, they won't even talk to the new woman in Dad's life. Sometimes they threaten never to speak to Dad again and never let him see his grandchildren. Some fathers succumb to this pressure, while others say, "I have a right to go on with my life. I don't like being lonely. I enjoy this woman's company and we are going to get married regardless of whether you approve or not. But it won't be me that terminates our relationship. That will be up to you." Some children choose never to speak to their father again and these dads soon come in to see me to revamp their estate plan. The bottom line: the new wife is in and the children are out. "Why should I leave anything to my daughter when she won't even talk to me?" one client said. "She said I no longer have a daughter. I'm just granting her wish."

Children step up to the plate when needed

Sometimes the Golden Years are not so golden when they arrive with mental and physical decline. As long as Mom and Dad are physically and mentally capable, they are fine. When Dad dies, Mom is still fine because she can care for herself. However, when a physical or mental problem surfaces, Mom may no longer be able to live alone, especially if she needs help with every daily task. Most children have never planned for this situation or thought about what they would do. They are busy raising their own families or may have just launched the last child out of the nest. It is the time when a married couple finally gets some peace in their life. They can travel and do some things they have never been able to do because of commitments with their children.

Suddenly they get a call from a neighbor, the hospital administrator, or the Department of Children and Families formerly known as HRS. "Mrs. Jones, I'm calling about your mother. She is not doing very well. She fell and broke her hip and has been hospitalized. She was in her house on the floor for ten hours before a neighbor found her. The Department of Children and Families has done an investigation and determined that she no longer has the 'capacity to consent' and can no longer make decisions regarding her financial matters and healthcare matters." As her only daughter, you are asked to come immediately to help her get her affairs in order.

For many grown children, a nuclear bomb blast couldn't be any more shocking. What do you do? Did Mom and Dad have an estate plan in place? Where do you get help? Does she have enough money to pay for her care? Does she have long-term care insurance? Does she have medical coverage? Where are the important papers? How do you write checks and pay for things? What do you do? You call your estate lawyer. You call me. After the legal work is completed and the daughter has been placed in control, she is in charge. The roles have changed and the daughter is now responsible for her mother. Most daughters (and sons) placed in this position take charge and make the changes in their lives to accommodate this new responsibility. Once the initial shock and confusion wears off, and Mom is settled, it becomes much easier. The remaining decisions concern how to continue to pay for her care and what treatment she should receive. If Mom has long-term health care insurance, the decisions are easy. Unfortunately, most seniors do not have this coverage. It is one of the fastest selling types of insurance but only a small percentage of seniors have it now.

The daughter reviews the finances and then liquidates assets to pay for the continuing care. Some seniors have enough ready cash and income to pay for assisted living or a nursing home. However, at an average cost of $5,000 per month (and rising), most do not.

The children then must seek professional help from an Elder Law Attorney or Estate Planning Attorney to get Mom qualified for Medicaid. In most states, Medicaid will pay for assisted living, but all states pay for nursing home care if Mom meets the qualifications of practically being destitute (Medicaid is a welfare program). Without going into great detail, Mom will qualify for Medicaid to pay the nursing home bills if she has less than about $1,600 in income and less than $2,000 in the bank. She can have a burial plan, $2,000 in cash value life insurance, a wedding ring of any value, a car, and a home of any value. The home will be excluded only if she or the one making application asserts that Mom intends to return home. If Mom got better (which we know she won't), she would certainly like to return to her home. There are many other legal issues I have skimmed over, such as the qualifications for Medicaid when Dad needs the nursing home, and Mom doesn't have enough money to pay the nursing home, and her monthly household bills.

My Story

First day at law school

My first day of law school I was sitting in the front row of the classroom, which, as I later learned, was not the best place to sit—you get picked on more often if you sit up front. Many professors are myopic and can only see things up close. During the first class, the Civil Procedure Professor, Mr. Paige, lectured on the rules of civil procedure. These are the rules that govern the civil side of court, as opposed to the rules that govern the criminal side. Filing requirements, time restrictions, and how you do things are all covered by the rules of civil procedure. Professor Paige was talking very energetically. He was a first year teacher and this was his second class on the first day. He desperately wanted to impart wisdom and understanding. I was concentrating intently and trying just as desperately to comprehend, hoping to absorb every word.

I was doing reasonably well until he said, "Now we are going to discuss bifurcated trials under the rubric of civil conflicts of interest." My mind instantly went into overload and simply shut down. I realized I didn't understand a word he just said and I was filled with self-doubt, wondering what the hell I was even doing here. I didn't have the foggiest idea what "bifurcated" or "rubric" meant, and the headache started immediately. At the same time, I started to itch under my arm-pits, which was not a good sign. The class droned on for another half hour, but I couldn't tell you anything else he said. I was in mental shock.

Thankfully, the bell rang at the end of the period and everyone got up and left the room for a 15 minute break before the next class. Still slightly shell-shocked, I wandered into the library where I found several of my classmates sitting around a library conference table, also looking shell-shocked.

One said, "What the hell is a 'rubric'?"

Another added, "I don't know, but it's probably related to something that's 'bifurcated.'"

A third guy asked plaintively, "Did anyone understand anything he said?"

As it turned out, no one had a clue what the professor had just spent 50 minutes talking about. If it was his job to scare the shit out of us and possibly weed out the fence sitters, he was successful. I heard three students dropped out of school the first day. Hearing the other classmates talk gave me a certain assurance and determination because I realized I was not a complete idiot. If I didn't understand what he said, probably most of the others didn't as well. There was hope for me yet.

Like my first day in law school, estate planning is initially confusing for most folks. However, you must do it. Estate planning doesn't happen all by itself. Remember, with a little work, patience, and perseverance, the understanding comes, and it all works out in the end. Gain a little knowledge, like you have reading this book, and then seek professional help to get your estate plan started. Good Luck.